THE IDEA OF THE NOVEL
IN THE EIGHTEENTH CENTURY

THE IDEA OF THE NOVEL
IN THE EIGHTEENTH CENTURY

Robert W. Uphaus

Editor

COLLEAGUES PRESS

1988

Studies in Literature, 1500–1800: No. 3

ISBN 0-937191-07-8
ISBN 0-937191-37-X (pb)
Library of Congress Catalog Card Number 88-71198
British Library Cataloguing-in-Publication data available
Copyright © 1988 by Colleagues Press Inc.

Published by Colleagues Press Inc.
Post Office Box 4007
East Lansing, MI 48826

Outside North America
Boydell and Brewer Ltd.
Post Office Box 9
Woodbridge, Suffolk IP12 3DF
England

Printed in the United States of America

CONTENTS

PREFACE

THE ESSAYS in this volume, all written for this specific occasion, address two interrelated questions: how was the novel conceived, read, and understood in the eighteenth century, and what kinds of critical approaches or methodologies (new and traditional) lead to a better understanding of the idea — really, ideas — of the novel in the eighteenth century?

Too often, what is either ignored or forgotten is that throughout the eighteenth century reading fiction was regarded as an inferior and oftentimes dangerous activity. The term "novel" itself carried with it many pejorative associations. There was great fear of what Samuel Johnson described as the novel's use of "promiscuous description," a fear too easily dismissed by those modern critics who celebrate such description as the source of the novel's power of "imitation." Those in the eighteenth century who did fear the novel, and there were many, did so on a variety of grounds. Initially, such fear was based on the assumption that the novel would become a rival (as it did) to traditional moral treatises, conduct books, educational manuals and even Scripture itself. Later in the century numerous periodicals condemned the habit of "novelism," principally on the basis that novels were an obstacle to moral improvement, and even so sophisticated a critic as Samuel Taylor Coleridge observed that reading novels should not so much "be called pass-time as kill-time."

Clearly the novel was viewed as a threatening if not alien element in eighteenth-century culture. As a new genre in the making, the novel challenged a broad range of expectations and assumptions and, in turn, developed some entirely new ways of understanding literature and life. Put another way, we need to understand, as a number of eighteenth-century readers did, that the novel was not always a passive reflection or mirror of eighteenth-century society. Rather, the novel presented authors with the opportunity to make, not just shape, reality. A strong case — stated by several of the essays in this volume — can be

vii

made that the eighteenth-century novel was formative or constitutive, not just representative, of reality.

In this volume, for example, John Richetti argues that "the eighteenth-century novel can be said to form part of an emerging social formation, connected at the least as a parallel phenomenon to an increasingly efficient ordering of objects and persons through written documents and records, as the organized totality called the nation-state begins to materialize" (p. 49). And, identifying the formative power of Maria Edgeworth's Rosamond stories, Mitzi Myers demonstrates how "Edgeworth replaces the usual heterosexual romance script fusing female self-definition with relations between the sexes by a mother-daughter educational narrative thematizing domestic realism and enlightened choice, dramatizing through its rationally mothered heroine's tutorial adventures how young readers can learn to cope with their culture" (p. 71).

Instead of making the customary assumption that a fiction-reading audience was in place and that it had somehow learned how to read the novel in a sophisticated "literary" way, all the essays in this volume raise anew questions that were asked by numerous eighteenth-century readers and writers. Some of the questions (or problems) are: What was the novel supposed to do? Was it just a vehicle of entertainment, or did it lay claim on the reader's public and private life? Where, in fact, did the novel rank in relation to other forms of reading? What were the novel's limitations—moral, religious, social, as well as literary? What were an author's responsibilities to his/her audience?

This volume considers these and many other questions in a variety of ways. The essays by Weinsheimer, Myers, and Richter tend to focus on reception and the formative influence of the novel on readers, especially women—who were the major consumers of fiction during most of the eighteenth century. Weinsheimer discusses the centrality of Samuel Johnson's essay, *Rambler* 4, juxtaposing it against what he calls complacent conceptions of reading. Against the backdrop of Johnson's fear that novels had the power "to figure or configure the mind. . .so that experience is processed in a particular way" (p. 5), Weinsheimer examines the significant consequences of Johnson's emphasis on critical judgment to "resist the violent effects which the force of example imposes on passive, impressionable minds" (p. 13).

Similarly, Myers and Richter, from different standpoints, focus on the formative influence of different kinds of fiction and on the reception of that fiction by women in particular. In the context of early juvenile fictions of female development, Myers examines Maria Edgeworth's Rosamond stories as a complex *Bildungsroman* that "enacts its author's as well as its protagonist's coming of age—mothering writer, heroine, and reader alike" (pp. 67-68). Arguing that Fanny Burney's prototypical novels of female development are "novels of nondevelopment . . .[that reiterate] feminine powerlessness," Myers contrasts Burney's female *Bildungsroman* with that of Maria Edgeworth, whose "double-voiced narrative juxtaposes the child's subjective point of view with the mother's instructive commentary and frames both within an enabling myth of the female author as maternal educator" (p. 74).

Just as Myers focuses on the female *Bildungsroman*, Richter discusses the evolution and reception of another kind of fiction—the Gothic novel—that was especially popular with women readers. Richter contends that the Gothic novel began in the late eighteenth century "in dialectical opposition to two other contemporary fictional forms, the didactic novel and the novel of manners" (p. 117). Employing a revised version of Hans Robert Jauss's ideas about reception and literary history, Richter views the Gothic novel as "at least partly the result of a complex interaction between producers and consumers, between authors on the one hand and audiences and publishers on the other" (p. 118). As part of his discussion, Richter argues for the existence of a split in the readership of the 1790s, out of which "the Gothic novel came in simultaneously with a new wave in reader response."

Where Weinsheimer, Myers, and Richter tend to emphasize the reception of eighteenth-century fiction, the essays by Beasley, Richetti, and Dussinger focus largely on formal problems—that is, matters relating to the shape, control, and coherence of the novel's internal properties. Beasley discusses how the early novel developed through "a process of self-conscious reciprocity" (p. 22). He further suggests that many authors "looked at the world from a common vantage point" (p. 22)—a thesis he pursues by considering how the episodic form of the eighteenth-century novel "provided some boundaries to the range of [the novelists'] vision and to the structures and meanings of their narratives" (p. 22). Observing that the problems of the early novelists were "epistemological as well as formal," Beasley suggests that "the desire to find meaning preceded the desire to create appropriate forms" (p. 25).

In like manner, Richetti takes up the central challenge for the early novelists of finding and representing meaning within the formal confines of the novel. Contrasting the eighteenth- with the nineteenth-century novel, Richetti argues that what eighteenth-century novels are about " is precisely the difficulty of imagining the ultimate social coherence that nineteenth-century novelists take for granted" (p. 47). Lacking such coherence, eighteenth-century narrative depicts "historically specific individuals . . . with a new clarity and insistence. Such figures are elaborately, pointedly derived from local and particularized social and historical circumstances rather than from the generalized moral essentialism of literary tradition" (pp. 49-50). Richetti inspects Defoe's fiction as a strong instance of how a fascination with the spectacle of trade stimulated Defoe's imagination into "recurring moments of totalizing social vision" (p. 52). In Richetti' view, Defoe's social vision dramatizes "the irresistible influence of large social structures and [evokes] at times a controlling if subterranean totality as the ground of the erratic and improvisational individualism they seem to celebrate" (p. 54).

Where Beasley and Richetti deal with the novelist's attempt at, and difficulty with, representing social comprehensiveness and coherence, Dussinger details how Jane Austen's use of free indirect discourse — otherwise known as *le style indirect libre* or *die erlebte Rede* — enables her not only to surmount technical novelistic problems, but powerfully establishes her "experimental zest for indirectly representing speech, [thus creating] a comic text with an astounding variety of illusory effects contributing to a character's 'presence' in narrative" (p. 111). By attending to Austen's experimental daring and the sometimes subversive effects of her style, Dussinger challenges the view of Austen as "the prototype of narrative as well as moral order in the history of the English novel" (p. 107), at the same time that he rejects the view of Austen as the representative of "the feminine half of the upper bourgeoisie who looked back nostalgically in a revolutionary age to the social and moral calm of the *ancien régime*" (p. 108).

Taken together the essays in this volume attend to the broad range of conditions of meaning during the time the early novel was conceived, produced, and received. As a whole, the essays offer a wideranging study of eighteenth-century authors, texts, and readers. Implicitly and explicitly, each essay inquires into the changes and continuities between the production and reception of the eighteenth-century novel and our modern understanding of these phenomena. Such a study of the idea of the novel engages all of us in the common enterprise we variously call meaning, understanding, and interpretation.

R. W. U.
East Lansing, Michigan

THE IDEA OF THE NOVEL
IN THE EIGHTEENTH CENTURY

FICTION AND THE FORCE OF EXAMPLE

Joel Weinsheimer

RAMBLER 4, Johnson's most intensive meditation on fiction, speaks to our deepest hope as students of the novel and humane letters generally: the hope, namely, that literature has a value beyond the gratification of curiosity and desire for pleasure. The new kind of fiction, Johnson argues, possesses value in proportion to its power; and its power, like that of history, consists in the force of example exercised upon its readers. For Johnson, the novel invites or, rather, demands scrutiny because it is dangerous. It cannot be perused with detached complacency because it has the capacity to make an impression and leave its mark on readers. The new fiction at its worst, he contends, embodies a particularly insidious, because imperceptible, form of violence: its art is the ethical equivalent of "murdering without pain."[1] For good or ill, novels have consequences and produce effects; they are not only imitative but potentially formative of the reader's experience, and that "efficacy" explains why they must be taken seriously.

That this characterization scarcely exaggerates Johnson's sense of concern can be demonstrated by comparing his account with other, more complacent conceptions of reading. Addison, for example, enjoins his reader "to make the Sphere of his innocent Pleasures as wide as possible, that he may retire into them with Safety. . . . Of this nature are those [pleasures] of the Imagination, which do not require such a Bent of Thought as is necessary to our more serious Employments . . . but, like a gentle Exercise to the Faculties, awaken them from Sloth and Idleness, without putting them upon any Labour or Difficulty."[2] Perhaps it was Addison's very success in tempting thousands to taste the easy pleasures of imaginative literature which brought home to Johnson, a half century later, how little innocuous and indeed how dangerous was the prevalence of imagination. What Addison had described as a safe and innocent

1

hobby seemed instead to Johnson a potent force, a power not to be taken
lightly.

Imagery Johnson defines in the *Dictionary* as "such descriptions as force
the image of the thing described upon the mind"; and emphasizing this
force, he praises Akenside's most famous poem, "The Pleasures of Imagination," because it "includes all images that can strike."[3] A striking
image is one that makes an impact and so leaves an impression or
imprint on the tablet of mind.[4] The danger of novels would be less if they
conveyed imageless precepts, as does moral philosophy. But they deal
rather in examples, and Johnson warns that "the power of example is so
great, as to take possession of the memory by a kind of violence, and
produce effects almost without intervention of the will." Examples
embodied in images have the potential for unconscious invasion, possession, subversion. With such images, he concludes, "care ought to be
taken."

In contrast to Johnson's concern, Addison's complacency results from
the fact that he restricts the effect of imaginative literature to delight and
credits it with no cognitive import, no significance as knowledge. "The
Pleasures of the Imagination [are not] . . . so refined as those of the
Understanding. The last are, indeed, more preferable, because they are
founded on some new Knowledge or Improvement in the Mind of
Man."[5] But the products of imagination, by contrast to those of understanding, impart no knowledge. Unlike Addison, Johnson need make no
apology for his interest in literature, since he considers it a product of
more than imagination. Thus he claims for the new fiction the full
breadth of value that Horace claimed for poetry. "Simul et jucunda et
idonea dicere vitae" is the motto of *Rambler* 4: at once pleasure and
suitability to tell of life. With that strong claim, Johnson begins his
essay: "The works of fiction, with which the present generation seems
more particularly delighted, are such as exhibit life in its true state."
They offer increased delight, and present increased danger, because this
fiction is true: it "tells of life." We recall that Johnson deplores the
depiction of morally mixed characters, "whose endowments threw a
brightness on their crimes, and whom scarcely any villainy made perfectly detestable." Yet he urges novelists to exclude such characters from
their fiction not because they are false but because they are true. "There
have been men indeed splendidly wicked" and they "have been in all ages
the great corrupters of the world." Though otherwise indefensible, morally ambiguous characters can at least claim to be "agreeable to observation and experience." Just that truth (and the efficacy deriving from it) is
the reason for banishing them from fiction, for without it they would be
of no concern.

Novels have cognitive value because they are true fictions. But that, in Johnson's view, does not distinguish them essentially from poems, since both are not only fictive but in principle true. The "comedy of romance," as Johnson (like Fielding[6]) labelled the new fiction, "is to be conducted nearly by the rules of comic poetry." And of poets Johnson wrote that they "profess fiction" (one thinks of Sidney who affirmed nothing), but he goes on to say that "the legitimate end of fiction is the conveyance of truth."[7] Whether in poetry or prose, fictive literature ideally possesses truth value: it has something to teach readers about themselves insofar as its authors are "just copyers of human manners." Since to be a novelist "requires, together with that learning which is to be gained from books, that experience which . . . must arise from general converse and accurate knowledge of the living world," novels offer the opportunity not only to receive pleasure but to acquire knowledge. With the knowledge of life that comes from both experience and books, novelists write the kind of experienceable books that are "idonea dicere vitae." They can serve as "introductions to life." But, most important to Johnson, the cognitive significance of novels is not merely that they yield factual "knowledge of the world" (which can be got from the world itself); fiction conveys the practical, applicable knowledge most worth having, "the knowledge of vice and virtue."

The power of novels derives from their imaging a true world, familiar and recognizable to shoemakers and philosophers alike. Moreover, because their authors are not "at liberty . . . to invent," and because they "exhibit life in its true state," comic romances qualify as a variety of history in Johnson's opinion. "Familiar histories," he terms them — just as he called his own fable *The History of Rasselas* — even though he says, too, that they are "narratives, where historical veracity has no place."[8] The fictiveness of the events and persons they represent does not, in Johnson's view, disqualify such narratives from being called histories precisely insofar as they are "familiar," that is, verisimilar to the common reader's sense of everyday experience. In the eighteenth century, it is important to remember, *story* and *history* were nearly synonymous, just as factual research and imaginative elaboration were not nearly so dichotomized as we would like to think they are today. The idea of the novel in the eighteenth century is closely allied to the idea of history and derives in large part from it.

When Addison considers reading history as one source of the pleasures of imagination, he characterizes it (predictably for "the Spectator") as an entertaining spectacle.

It is the most agreeable Talent of an Historian to draw up his Armies and fight his Battels in proper Expressions, to set before our Eyes the Divisions, Cabals, and Jealousies of Great Men. . . . We love to see the Subject unfolding itself by just Degrees, and breaking upon us insensibly, that so we may be kept in a pleasing Suspence. . . . [Livy] describes every thing in so lively a Manner, that his whole History is like an admirable Picture, and . . . his Reader becomes a kind of Spectator.[9]

Hume too thinks of history as spectacle, and history readers as spectators: "what more agreeable entertainment to the mind, than to . . . see all [the] human race, from the beginning of time, pass, as it were, in review before us? . . . What spectacle can be imagined, so magnificent, so various, so interesting? What amusement, either of the senses or imagination, can be compared with it?"[10] To Hume's rhetorical questions, Johnson gives an unexpected answer in *Rasselas*, chapter 6, where the delights of spectating are compared to those of flying. "You, sir," the projector bubbles enthusiastically to Rasselas, "will easily conceive with what pleasure a philosopher, furnished with wings, and hovering in the sky, would see the earth, and all it's inhabitants, rolling beneath him. . . . How must it amuse the pendent spectator to see the moving scene of land and ocean, cities and desarts!"[11] When this latter-day Icarus falls into the water, we get the point. Rising to the heights of distanced spectation is not possible for human beings, who must necessarily see what they can from their limited vantage here below. Since, like all of us, historians must remain immersed in history, they are susceptible to being infected by it, and the distance which creates the spectacle by dividing it from the spectator collapses. Even to think of historical detachment as an ideal is to deny what history really is: "The examples and events of history," Johnson says, "press, indeed, upon the mind with the weight of truth."[12]

Just as historical events engender a train of consequences in which even bystanders and spectators get caught up involuntarily and are overwhelmed, so also and no less powerfully, Johnson suggests, historical examples press upon the minds of history-readers and produce effects almost without intervention of the will. Between the force of personally experienced events and the force of narrated examples, between the effects of living and the effects of reading history books there are real differences. But history does not become impotent when it is written down. It alters but retains its capacity to register an effect and leave a mark. "Familiar histories" which "exhibit life in its true state," novels such as Fielding's *History of a Foundling* and Richardson's *History of a Young Lady*, are a mode of power.

Such histories can affect material events indirectly, but first and primarily, as Johnson says, their power is displayed as pressure upon the mind. "Impression," therefore, is one term given to the mental effect of books. "Turn" is another. Leonora, the widow in Addison's *Spectator* 37, has directed all her passions to "a love of Books and Retirement. . . . As her Reading has lain very much among Romances, it has given her a very particular Turn of Thinking."[13] For romances to turn thinking is for them to figure or configure the mind (as we would say of computers) so that experience is processed in a particular way. Reading "histories" of heroic romance gives Leonora's mind a turn in the sense of a particular bent, slant, or bias — to borrow the term from lawn bowling — so everything rolls in the same direction.

Arabella, heroine of Charlotte Lennox's *The Female Quixote*, exhibits this same inclination and for the same reason. As Addison's Leonora has filled her vacant hours with such French romances as *Cassandra*, *Cleopatra*, and *Clelia*, Lennox's Arabella finds precisely these books "a most pleasing Entertainment." But their effect, we find, was not merely pleasure, for Arabella's "Ideas . . . and the Objects around her had taken a romantic Turn; and supposing Romances were real pictures of Life, from them she drew all her notions and expectations. . . . Her mind being wholly filled with the most extravagant Expectations, she was alarmed by every trifling incident; and kept in a continual anxiety by a Vicissitude of Hopes, Fears, Wishes, and Disappointments."[14] Arabella's "romantic turn" displays itself not only in the slant she gives to "objects around her"; her perceptions are governed, more fundamentally, by her expectations — and they, in turn, are governed by her reading. Arabella takes romances to be histories; and the effect produced by her reading them is precisely the patterning of expectation that was generally considered to be the effect of reading history.

In his *Letters on the Study and Use of History*, for example, Bolingbroke explains that through history "the temper of the mind is formed, and a certain turn given to our ways of thinking." Everything we experience thereafter will be affected by "the temper of mind, and the turn of thought, that we have acquired beforehand, and bring along with us."[15] Since Arabella believes romances to be "real Pictures of Life," she quite properly educates her expectations through them; and rather than naively approaching experience with a tabula rasa, she brings to perception a mind already projecting and anticipating. It is only *what* she projects — namely, heroic adventure — that makes her quixotic; the mechanism of projection itself has nothing ridiculous about it.

"*Don Quixote*," Ronald Paulson states, "is by all odds the most seminal narrative satire of the seventeenth and eighteenth centuries."[16] One reason for the pervasiveness of Cervantes' influence is that his novel focuses precisely on the capacity of reading to form the reader's experience, for better or worse, by affecting patterns of expectation. In *Rambler* 2, for instance, after recounting the Don's wildly impractical hopes and desires, Johnson nevertheless concludes that, however fantastical Don Quixote's dreams, "very few readers, amidst their mirth or pity, can deny that they have admitted visions of the same kind. . . . Our hearts inform us that he is not more ridiculous than ourselves, except that he tells what we have only thought."[17] Reading Cervantes is like reading biography: the reader discovers that "we are all prompted by the same motives, all deceived by the same fallacies [and] all animated by hope."[18] All, we might add, are like the Knight of the Woeful Countenance in that our reading not only recapitulates our experiences but formulates our hopes and gives us something to desire. Apart from this formative power, literature becomes merely the innocuous entertainment that Addison thought. In *Rambler* 4, Johnson characterizes heroic romance as just this kind of harmless amusement: "In the romances formerly written, every transaction and sentiment was so remote from all that passes among men, that the reader was in very little danger of making any applications to himself; the virtues and crimes were equally beyond his sphere of activity." By reason of its giants and knights, castles and deserts, the old fiction was inoffensive but also inapplicable, ineffectual, and thus without ethical significance. Its danger is small because, Johnson asserts, "what we cannot credit we shall never imitate."

But the relation between belief and imitation is not so patent as Johnson here makes it seem, and it deserves closer attention. Here Bolingbroke is again of service, for Johnson's contention that readers will not imitate what they do not believe has a close precedent in the fifth of the *Letters on the Study and Use of History*. The subject of Bolingbroke's disdain is ancient history, which he considers no less unbelievable and insignificant than heroic romance.

> We are apt naturally to apply to ourselves what has happened to other men, and . . . examples take their force from hence; as well those which history, as those which experience, offers to our reflection. What we do not believe to have happened, therefore, we shall not thus apply. . . . Ancient history . . . is quite unfit therefore in this respect to answer the ends that every reasonable man should propose to himself in this study; because such ancient history will never gain sufficient credit with any reasonable man. . . . When imagination grows lawless and wild, rambles out of the precincts of nature, and tells of heroes and giants, fairies and enchanters . . . reason does not connive a moment; but, far from receiving such narrations as historical, she rejects them as unworthy to be placed even among the fabulous. . . .

Nothing less than enthusiasm and phrensy can give credit to such histories, or apply such examples. Don Quixote believed; but even Sancho doubted.[19]

This last sentence points up the essential problem. It may be, as Johnson and Bolingbroke both contend, that application depends on belief, but "Don Quixote believed." So also Arabella, the female quixote, believed; she accepted romance as history. It would seem, then, that the difference between comic and heroic romance, that is, between credible and incredible fiction, cannot be fixed with any precision.

Though for Johnson heroic romance deals in manifestly fictitious events and feelings remote from those familiar to the reader, even he acknowledges that there is an "act of imagination, that realizes the event however fictitious, or approximates it however remote."[20] Fed on romance, the imagination of Rasselas functions this way when "he feigned to himself an orphan virgin robbed of her little portion by a treacherous lover. . . . So strongly was the image impressed upon his mind, that he started up in the maid's defence, and ran forward to seize the plunder with all the eagerness of real persuit."[21] Moreover, though Johnson had written that the reader is in little danger from heroic romance, he adds to the lineage of Addison's Leonora and Lennox's Arabella, a cautionary character of his own: one Imperia, who "having spent the early part of her life in the perusal of romances, brought with her into the gay world all the pride of Cleopatra; [and] expected nothing less than vows, altars, and sacrifices."[22] Clearly, Johnson at least entertained the idea that, however lawless and wild, even the old heroic romance had the potential for altering the schemata of the reader's hopes and fears.

For this reason, it cannot be surprising that *The Female Quixote*, which dramatizes that potential, was almost certainly written in part by Johnson.[23] The premise of this novel, like that of Cervantes, is that no narrative, however improbable, can be considered ipso facto incredible, harmless, and incapable of influence. Every novel therefore carries the danger of distorting the reader's pattern of expectations in the same way as Arabella's. In the climactic chapter describing her recovery, Arabella's therapy comes in the form of sound logic from a (very Johnsonian) "good divine," who tells her, "It is the Fault of the best Fictions that they teach young Minds to expect strange Adventures and sudden vicissitudes."[24] The damage consists not in the fact that novels produce expectations but in the silly things that Arabella has learned to expect. Thus the doctor must convince her not only that heroic romances are fictions (not histories) but that they are "absurd" and should not be believed—that a "long

Life may be passed without a single Occurrence that can cause much Surprize, or produce any unexpected Consequence of great Importance."[25] Certainly the unexpected happens on occasion, but it is folly to expect it.

Since the authors of Arabella's romances must have been aware that their tales were absurd, the doctor concludes that "to be credited . . . seems not to be the Hope or Intention of these Writers."[26] But cannot this incredibility, and the moral insignificance that is its consequence, be affirmed not just of absurd fiction but of all fiction? Arabella draws this inference in her reply: "he that writes without Intention to be credited, must write to little Purpose; for what Pleasure or Advantage can arise from Facts that never happened? What Examples can be afforded by the Patience of those who never suffered, or the Chastity of those who were never solicited? The great End of History, is to shew how much human Nature can endure or perform."[27] These are legitimate questions, one must admit, for it seems impossible that fictional narratives lacking in historical veracity could, in the very similar words of *Rambler* 4, "teach us what we may hope and what we may perform."

In a passage obviously written by Lennox, the doctor addresses this issue:

> Truth is not always injured by Fiction. An admirable Writer of our own Time [i.e., Richardson], has found the Way to convey the most solid Instructions, the noblest Sentiments, and the most exalted Piety, in the pleasing Dress of a Novel, and, to use the Words of the greatest Genius in the present Age [i.e., Johnson], "Has taught the Passions to move at the Command of Virtue." The Fables of Aesop, though never I suppose believed, yet have been long considered as Lectures of moral and domestic Wisdom.[28]

The doctor does not explain how *fictional* examples which elicit no belief can have any *real* effect; he merely asserts that it happens and has always happened. But the explanation is not far to seek, for its analogue is to be found in a familiar passage of Johnson's "Preface to Shakespeare": "It will be asked, how the drama moves, if it is not credited. It is credited with all the credit due a drama." Transposed to narrative, this assertion has the interesting consequence that educational power cannot be confined to factual history alone. If Richardson's novels can teach because they are credited with all the credit due novels, and Aesop can teach by reason of the credit due to fables, then, judged in terms of potential educational impact, history and story are of equal value, equal applicability, and therefore equal moral significance.

Both command the field of practical truths applicable to life. But fiction is in one important respect superior to history since fiction without factuality can still be true. In that case, as Arabella explains, "the truth lies in the Application," though not in the story.[29] But when, conversely, history forfeits its claim to be applicable in order to exhibit mere facts, facts which do not press upon the mind with the weight of truth, then history — however factually accurate — degenerates into something like falsehood. For "between falsehood and useless truth," Johnson writes, "there is little difference."[30] John Vance's recent book, *Samuel Johnson and the Sense of History*, offers an eloquent demonstration, if any is needed, that Johnson was scarcely deficient in the historical sense. Yet there can be no doubt that Johnson despised the kind of history that "carried one away from common life, leaving no ideas behind which could serve *living wight* as warning or direction."[31] Insofar as it attempts to distinguish itself from the forms and ethical purposes of the novel, factual history can justify its claim to our assent and belief but not to our attention. Johnson was not alone in the opinion that some facts, those without the force of example, are not worth knowing. As he asserts that "all useless science is an empty boast,"[32] so Bolingbroke asserts that "application to any study that tends neither directly nor indirectly to make us better men and better citizens, is at best a specious and ingenious sort of idleness."[33] If the novel and history were to be defensible, the humanist had to show that both have something useful — something not just theoretical but applicable and practical — to teach.

Philosophy too could claim moral and educational value, and thus Bolingbroke often repeats the ancient maxim that "History is philosophy teaching by examples." Yet more than philosophy incarnate, he argues, history gives the force to philosophical precepts that they lack of themselves. "The examples which we find in history, improved by the lively descriptions . . . of historians will have a much better and more permanent effect than . . . the dry ethics of mere philosophy."[34] In the context of this same distinction of story from philosophy, Johnson writes of novels that "these familiar histories may perhaps be made of greater use than the solemnities of professed morality, and convey the knowledge of vice and virtue with more efficacy than axioms and definitions." The reason for their superior efficacy is that, as Bolingbroke explains, "Example appeals not to our understanding alone, but to our passions likewise. Example . . . sets passion on the side of judgment, . . . which is more than the strongest reasoning and clearest demonstration can do."[35] Insofar as philosophy remains ineffective without historical examples, including those of fictional history, to that extent novelistic history which "moves" the reader supersedes philosophy and remedies its deficiencies.

"Now, to improve by examples," Bolingbroke continues, "is to improve by imitation."[36] The habit of recalling the examples of history "will soon produce the habit of imitating them."[37] Along the same lines, as we have already noted, Johnson conceives of novelistic examples as eliciting imitation. He explains the impulse to imitation not by recourse to what we would call empathy, or community of feeling, but rather by appeal to commonality of situation, or what he calls "the universal drama." Just as in universal history spectacle is not divided from the spectator, so also in the universal drama the protagonist acts in the same play in which the audience too has a part. Thus "the young spectators fix their eyes upon him with closer attention, and hope by observing his behaviour and success to regulate their own practices, when they shall be engaged in the like part." In "universal drama" no one is a mere spectator, nor are the represented scenes mere spectacle, for in them readers and characters alike are equally involved. The protagonist whom the reader meets in this "mock encounter" therefore is not just a character but an example, an exemplary character, a hero, a model to be imitated when the reader finds himself in the same situation.

The traditional objection to this classical account of imitative learning is that "like" parts are never like enough for the reader to be able to profit from precedent or example. With some justice, Bolingbroke observes, "as to particular modes of actions, and measures of conduct, which the customs of different countries, the manners of different ages, and the circumstances of different conjunctures, have appropriated, as it were; it is always ridiculous, or imprudent and dangerous to employ them [as models]."[38] To the objection that special circumstances always preclude learning by imitation, there are several possible replies. One is that since particulars are so various, the would-be imitator must rise to the "spirit" or the general principle implied by them, that is, abstract from particulars the general precept which, by reason of its generality, can encompass the present situation as well as that of the past. In *The Serious Call*, William Law — another great teacher by examples — advocates something like this process when he urges readers to imitate the exemplary life of "Miranda."

> Some persons perhaps, who admire the purity and perfection of this life of Miranda, may say, how can it be proposed as a common example? how can we who are married, or we who are under the direction of our parents, imitate such a life?
>
>   It is answered, — just as you may imitate the life of our blessed Saviour and his Apostles. The circumstances of our Saviour's life, and the state and conditions of his Apostles, were more different from your's than that of

Miranda's is; and yet their life, the purity and the perfection of their behaviour, is the common example that is proposed to all christians.

It is their spirit therefore, their piety, their love of God, that you are to
imitate, and not the particular form of their life.[39]

Law will not allow his readers to escape the duty of imitation by pleading
difference of circumstances. But his way of enforcing that duty leads
back to the primacy of the precept, and in fact obviates the need for the
very examples by which he teaches. For if the purpose of studying
examples is to abstract a moral generality in the end, one might as well
begin with the abstractions in the first place. Thus we are left in a
quandary: abstract religious maxims, like abstract philosophical precepts, lack the motivating force of concrete narrative examples; but
concrete examples, such as those of fictive and factual history, cannot be
transferred insofar as they are concrete.

To this quandary Bolingbroke offers a solution — one that is relevant
to Johnson's conception of the novel as well. Bolingbroke realizes that
history cannot be reduced to philosophy or abstract doctrine. The examples of history consist in concrete particulars, and those who propose to
learn from them must learn from their particularity and detail: "History
. . . of all kinds, of civilized and uncivilized, of ancient and modern
nations, in short, all history that descends to a sufficient detail of human
actions and characters, is useful to bring us acquainted with our species,
nay, with ourselves."[40] But this richness of particularity does not preclude
learning by imitation; it precludes only copying. Any learning through
the imitation of historical particulars necessitates recognition of historical difference. Imitation thus involves a process that Bolingbroke likens
to translation: "History is the ancient author: experience is the modern
language. We form our taste on the first, we translate the sense and
reason, we transfuse the spirit and force; but we imitate only the particular graces of the original; we imitate them according to the idiom of our
own tongue, that is, we substitute often equivalents in the lieu of them,
and are far from affecting to copy them servilely."[41] The process of
imitative translation requires a self-critical awareness of the particularity
of one's own time and circumstances as well as those of the other. Thus
imitation does not necessitate abstracting the general from the particular; rather, it relates particular to particular in a way that discovers
continuity across historical distance and similarity in difference.

Though Johnson, Bolingbroke, and Lennox alike caution against
uncritical imitation, none of them doubts the basic Aristotelian thesis
that imitative learning is possible, fundamental, and profoundly important. One difference between man and the animals, Aristotle says (*Poetics*

4.2), is that man "is the most imitative of living creatures, and through imitation he learns his earliest lessons." Johnson repeats this observation in *Rambler* 135: "It is impossible to take a view on any side, or observe any of the various classes that form the great community of the world, without discovering the influence of example, and admitting with new conviction the observation of Aristotle, that 'man is an imitative animal.'" This general and basic imitativeness underlies Aristotle's definition of tragedy as the imitation of an action: it is not accidental that both drama and learning by example are forms of mimesis. Following Aristotle,[42] Johnson can say both that "the greatest excellency of art [is] to *imitate* nature" and that "what we cannot credit we shall never *imitate*." These are not homonyms to be distinguished in meaning. The reception and the production of literature are two forms of one process. At its most effective, Johnson suggests, art is imitation that generates imitations, for imitation is not only the essence of art but its end.

The idea that in its two manifestations imitation is one and continuous meets with resistance primarily because a dichotomy popularized by Edward Young has become firmly entrenched in critical discourse: "Imitations are of two kinds; one of nature, one of authors: the first we call original, and confine the term imitation to the second."[43] But against Young's distinction we might consider the alternative posed by Johnson's non-differentiation. The process by which people imitate other people whom they take as models is fundamentally continuous with the process by which the novelist imitates people. That the medium of the one is deeds, and that of the other words, should not hide their underlying continuity; conceding that, one discovers other continuities of imitation as well. The characters in novels, one might say in loosely Aristotelian fashion, are imitations of people. Lady Mary Wortley Montague, for example, said that Lennox's Arabella was modelled on Lady Hertford, later Duchess of Somerset.[44] Perhaps so, but novels also imitate other novels, as is especially evident in the case of *The Female Quixote*; it would be difficult to determine whether Arabella was imitated from the life or from a novel, or from both. Moreover, though characters may be considered imitations of people, Lennox's novel dramatizes the idea that people also imitate characters in novels. There is no doubt that people do at times imitate novels, often in the most literal fashion and with the most pathetic effects — as attested by the epidemic of suicides in 1774 following the publication of Goethe's *Werther*. So also a statistical correlation has been shown to exist between actual suicides publicized in the media and an increased suicide rate during the week thereafter.[45] In the eighteenth century and before, it was already evident that it makes no difference whether the event is fictional or historical: once known, it will draw imitators.

But the fact is that not everyone will imitate it, and that fact leaves an opening to argue that the power of example is not always so great as, in Johnson's words, to "produce effects almost without the intervention of the will." Johnson too valued distanced, critical reading as evident in the *Lives of the Poets* and in all his critical pronouncements. Deliberative, self-conscious judgment, and not unreflective immersion, characterizes his interpretive practice. Johnson's criticism is, in the strong sense of the word, critical. In *Rambler* 4 he rejects the notion that people are "grateful in the same degree as they are resentful" because it disregards the possibility of rational self-control. On the grounds of this same possibility, he limits his thesis that examples take involuntary possession of the reader's memory specifically to those readers whose will is too weak and whose knowledge is too narrow to exercise choice among examples to imitate. To both writers and readers, conscious, critical judgment is what Johnson advocates and practices, not least in *Rambler* 4 itself. Those capable of exercising such judgment can resist the violent effects which the force of example imposes on passive, impressionable minds.

These latter, Johnson suggests, are primarily "the young, the ignorant, and the idle" — like Lennox's Arabella. "The surprising Adventures with which [romances] were filled, proved a most pleasing Entertainment to a *young* Lady, who was *wholly secluded* from the World; [and] who had *no other Diversion*, but ranging like a Nymph through Gardens."[46] Similarly, we are not surprised that young, ignorant, and idle Tom Sawyer would prove susceptible to Dumas. Or, to illustrate the point with a nonfictional reader (does it matter?), Hannah More relates in her *Memoirs* the following conversation with Johnson:

> I alluded rather flippantly, I fear, to some witty passage in Tom Jones: he replied, "I am shocked to hear you quote from so vicious a book. I am sorry to hear you have read it: a confession which no modest lady should ever make. I scarcely know a more corrupt work." I thanked him for his correction; assured him I thought full as ill of it now as he did, and had only read it at an age when I was more subject to be caught by the wit, than able to discern the mischief.[47]

Because of her youth, More says, she was "subject to be caught." That subjection — the idea that, for the young, reading is not a reflective action but a passion — has since Plato (*Republic*, Book 2) been the rationale for control and censorship aimed at ensuring that the "best examples only are exhibited" to those unable to protect themselves. It is primarily children who are offered as evidence for this argument.[48] As Johnson says, "[Novels] are the entertainment of minds unfurnished with ideas, and therefore easily susceptible of impressions; not fixed by principles, and therefore easily following the current of fancy; not informed by experience, and consequently open to every false suggestion and partial account."

But it would be a mistake to think that Johnson posits any landmark of maturity beyond which false suggestions and partial accounts become ineffectual. Finite minds never become so fraught with knowledge, so furnished with ideas and fixed by principles, that they are impervious to subsequent impressions. Moreover, there is no point beyond which learning becomes unnecessary; and private experience, however much we acquire, is never sufficient but always in need of supplementation. That insufficiency of private experience justifies learning from books, late in life as well as early. To become eminent in any part of knowledge, Johnson argues in *Rambler* 154, "the first task is to study books, the next to contemplate nature. [The student] must first possess himself of the intellectual treasures which the diligence of former ages has accumulated, and then endeavor to encrease them by his own collections. The mental disease of the present generation, is impatience of study, contempt of the great masters of ancient wisdom, and a disposition to rely wholly upon unassisted genius."[49] This not uncommon defense of reading is fundamental to the humanist tradition. "How great soever a genius may be," Bolingbroke writes, "certain it is that he will never shine with the full lustre, nor shed the full influence he is capable of, unless to his own experience he adds the experience of other men and ages."[50] Burke, too, is "afraid to put men to live and trade each on his own private stock of reason; because we suspect that this stock in each man is small, and that the individuals would do better to avail themselves of the general bank and capital of nations, and of ages."[51] Private reason, individual genius, personal experience are at every stage of life in need of augmentation from the store of wisdom to be found in history.

But in defense of history Bolingbroke is not content with demonstrating the capacity of reading to expand one's horizons; he also calls attention to the inability of experience to do so:

> History prepares us for experience, and guides us in it [since history remedies the narrowness which our] experience for the most part rather confirms than removes: because it is for the most part confined. . . . Experience is doubly defective; we are born too late to see the beginning, and we die too soon to see the end of many things. History supplies both these defects.[52]

The study of history is always necessary insofar as personal experience is irremediably finite, and the intrinsic limitations of experience tend rather to confirm and deepen than to remove the prejudices of provincialism. Further, experience is sometimes unsafe. Johnson repeats Sidney's story of the painter who joined the battle so he could paint it better, "but his knowledge was useless for some mischievous sword took away his hand."[53] Bolingbroke cites Polybius to affirm that "since [personal experience] exposes us to great labor and peril whilst [reading history] works the same good effect, . . . the study of history is the best school."[54] Again, the doctor tells Arabella (in words that Johnson probably penned), "the great Use of Books, is that of participating without Labour or Hazard [in] the Experience of others."[55]

Something more than expanding the limits of private experience is involved in such statements. On this account, the purpose of books is not merely to increase the quantity of the reader's experiences but indeed to decrease it by obviating the need for some of them, the dangerous ones. Or, at least, the end of reading is to dissipate the force of actual personal experience by enabling the reader to undergo certain storied experiences — "mock encounters," Johnson calls them — the effect of which is, like an injection, to immunize the reader against the harm that would attend actual experiences of the same kind. "The purpose of these writings," Johnson states of the new fiction, "is surely not only to show mankind, but to provide that they may be seen hereafter with less hazard." And so too the doctor says to Arabella, "It is of little Importance . . . to decide whether in the real or fictitious Life, most Wickedness is to be found. Books ought to supply an Antidote to Example."[56] Books of fiction, Johnson clearly means, ought ideally to offer not just a supplement but an antidote to real personal experience. The great benefit of novels is to blunt the harmful impact of real, personally experienced examples by substituting for them fictive examples that are less harmful but no less powerful in their educative impact. Fiction offers an antidote to life.

Considered in this way, novels can never be judged exclusively by how closely they imitate life. "Being approved as just copyers of human manners, is not the most important concern that an author of this sort ought to have before him." If works of fiction do not merely imitate but ideally alter their readers' manner of life, then life cannot be the sole standard by which such books are evaluated. Quite the contrary, life is also to be judged by how closely it imitates the "familiar histories" that "convey the knowledge of vice and virtue." Especially for the Christian Johnson, life at its best is modelled on The Book, and there is always an appeal open from perception to principle. It needs "to be steadily inculcated, that virtue is the highest proof of understanding . . . and that vice is the natural consequence of narrow thoughts" because such moral truths, however necessary to be applied to life, cannot be derived from it. "It is therefore not a sufficient vindication of . . . a narrative, that the train of events is agreeable to observation and experience, for that observation which is called knowledge of the world, will be found much more frequently to make men cunning than good." Insofar as nature is fallen and the world is worldly, insofar as life is "discolored by passion" and "deformed by wickedness," mimetic fiction that merely "follows nature" and is "agreeable to observation and experience" teaches what is expedient and at best what is prudent. But to learn what is positively good one needs nonmimetic representations — or, more precisely, not representations of general nature but of those rare natures that embody the "most perfect idea of virtue" possible for human beings. In the imitation of uncommon exemplars lies the highest value of fiction. In imitating rare virtue, fiction provides an antidote to general, indiscriminate experience and, by the power of the exemplary to evoke imitation, it inculcates not only the knowledge of virtue but the desire to practice it.

To us, no doubt, these are mostly alien notions, though we can nevertheless recognize something not only vigorous and admirable but familiar in them. Johnson's multifaceted claim — that the novel is a vehicle of moral knowledge, that it conveys the knowledge of vice and virtue which experience alone cannot give and which reason based on axioms and definitions cannot make effectual, that it elicits imitation by the force of example, that it inculcates a kind of truth having the power to alter, for better or worse, the way people think and act — survived eighteenth-century satire of the imitators of romance and also romantic devaluations of imitation. It has survived allegations that art has no cognitive or moral significance, and outlasted attempts to divide what literature is from what it does.[57] This endurance does not validate Johnson's humanistic claim that literature is an effective force, but any denial of it must ultimately subvert the justification for literary study itself.

Notes

1 Subsequent quotations without references are all cited from *Rambler* 4, in *The Rambler, The Yale Works of Samuel Johnson*, ed. W. J. Bate and Albrecht B. Strauss (New Haven: Yale University Press, 1969), 3:19–25.

2 Joseph Addison, *The Spectator*, ed. Donald F. Bond, 5 vols. (Oxford: Clarendon Press, 1965), No. 411, 3:539.

3 "Akenside," *Lives of the English Poets*, ed. G. B. Hill, 3 vols. (1905; New York: Octagon, 1967), 3:417.

4 On the effect of images, see Susan Griffin's comment, "One cannot over-estimate the effect of images on our lives. . . . The human mind has a capacity beyond our conscious understanding to take in and imitate what it sees. The body silently memorizes all that it sees and the mind can accurately reproduce any images. . . . And no image we have ever seen leaves our minds. What we see does become a part of us." In *Pornography and Silence: Culture's Revenge against Nature* (New York: Harper and Row, 1981).

5 *The Spectator*, No. 411, 3:537–538. In "Samuel Johnson and Reader-Response Criticism," *The Eighteenth Century: Theory and Interpretation* 21 (1980): 94, Leopold Damrosch, Jr. points to "the fundamental gap between Johnson and almost any modern theorist. Putting it bluntly, he sees literature as cognitive as well as effective." Among modern theorists, Hans-Georg Gadamer is one of the few exceptions to the general denial of cognitive import to literature.

6 Robert E. Moore shows that Johnson's standards for the novel are better realized in Fielding's fiction than Richardson's, though Johnson defended Richardson against Fielding often, intensely, and sometimes unfairly. "Dr. Johnson on Fielding and Richardson," *PMLA* 66 (1951): 162–181.

7 "Dryden," *Lives*, 1:271.

8 Johnson's *Dictionary* makes no clear distinction between history as story and as narrative of proven facts. Lennard Davis is particularly instructive on this kind of non-differentiation in *Factual Fictions: The Origins of the English Novel* (New York: Columbia University Press, 1983), esp. ch. 3, "News/ Novels: The Undifferentiated Matrix." For a fully developed exposition of Johnson's conception of history, see John A. Vance, *Samuel Johnson and the Sense of History* (Athens: University of Georgia Press, 1984).

9 *The Spectator*, No. 420, 3:574.

10 *Essays Moral, Political and Literary*, 2:398–90. Cited by D. J. Womersley, "Lord Bolingbroke and Eighteenth-Century Historiography," *The Eighteenth Century: Theory and Interpretation* 28 (1987): 228.

11 *Samuel Johnson: "Rasselas," Poems, and Selected Prose*, ed. Bertrand Bronson, 3rd ed. (San Francisco: Rinehart, 1958), p. 619.

12 *Idler* 84, *The Yale Works*, 2:262.

13 *The Spectator*, No. 37, 1:158.

14 Charlotte Lennox, *The Female Quixote, or The Adventures of Arabella*, ed. Margaret Dalziel (London: Oxford University Press, 1970), p. 7.

15 *The Works of Lord Bolingbroke*, 4 vols. (London: Cass, 1967), 2:182.

16 *Satire and the Novel in Eighteenth-Century England* (New Haven: Yale University Press, 1967), p. 33.

17 *Yale Works of Samuel Johnson*, 3:11.

18 *Rambler* 60, *The Yale Works of Samuel Johnson*, 3:320.

19 *The Works of Lord Bolingbroke*, 2:211–212.

20 *Rambler* 60, *The Yale Works of Samuel Johnson*, 3:318.

21 *Samuel Johnson*, ed. Bronson, p. 615.

22 *Rambler* 115, *The Yale Works of Samuel Johnson*, 4:252.

23 In her notes (pp. 414–415) to *The Female Quixote*, Dalziel follows John Mitford's article (*The Gentleman's Magazine*, 1843) in accepting this attribution. But see Duncan Isles's denial of it in the appendix to the Dalziel edition, p. 418.

24 *The Female Quixote*, p. 379.

25 Ibid.

26 Ibid., p. 376.

27 Ibid.

28 Ibid., p. 377.

29 Compare the notion of truth in Johnson's comments on Gray's *The Bard*: "we are improved only as we find something to be imitated or declined. I do not see that *The Bard* promotes any truth, moral or political." "Gray," *Lives*, 3:438. For the humanist, Thomas Seebohm explains, "Truth is, in the case of philosophy as well as in jurisprudence, the sciences, and poetry, that which surfaces in the process of application in concrete situations. Thus the wisdom of the humanist is higher than the philosopher's wisdom." In "The End of Philosophy: Three Historical Aphorisms," *Hermeneutics and Deconstruction*, ed. Hugh J. Silverman and Don Ihde (Albany: State University of New York Press, 1985), p. 18.

30 *Idler* 84, *The Yale Works of Samuel Johnson*, 2:262.

31 Hester Lynch Piozzi, *Anecdotes of the Late Samuel Johnson* (New York: Garland, 1974), p. 80.

32 *Rambler* 83, *The Yale Works of Samuel Johnson*, 4:70.

33 *The Works of Lord Bolingbroke*, 2:177.

34 Ibid., p. 183.

35 Ibid., p. 178.

36 Ibid., p. 193.

37 Ibid., p. 178.

38 Ibid., p. 194.

39 *A Serious Call to a Devout and Holy Life Adapted to the State and Condition of All Orders of Christians*, 20th ed. (Romsey, Hants: William Sharp, 1816), p. 106.

40 *The Works of Lord Bolingbroke*, 2:228–229.

41 Ibid., p. 194.

42 See John Boyd, *The Function of Mimesis and Its Decline* (Cambridge: Harvard University Press, 1968); and John Draper, "Aristotelian 'Mimesis' in Eighteenth-Century England," *PMLA* 36 (1926): 372–400.

43 *Conjectures on Original Composition* (Leeds: Scolar Press, 1966), p. 9.

44 See *The Female Quixote*, p. 389.

45 David P. Phillips, "The Influence of Suggestion on Suicide," *American Sociological Review* 39 (1974): 340–354.

46 *The Female Quixote*, p. 7. Italics added.

47 Cited by Robert E. Moore, "Dr. Johnson on Fielding and Richardson," p. 163.

48 For Victorian thought on this topic, see Patrick Dunae, "Penny Dreadfuls: Late Nineteenth-Century Boys' Literature and Crime," *Victorian Studies* 22 (1979): 133–150.

49 *Yale Works of Samuel Johnson*, 5:56.

50 *The Works of Lord Bolingbroke*, 2:179.

51 *Reflections on the Revolution in France*, ed. Conor Cruise O'Brien (Baltimore: Penguin, 1968), p. 183.

52 Ibid., pp. 183 and 186.

53 *The Letters of Samuel Johnson*, ed. R. W. Chapman (Oxford: Clarendon Press, 1953), 3:69.

54 *The Works of Lord Bolingbroke*, 2:184.

55 *The Female Quixote*, p. 386.

56 Ibid., p. 388.

57 For example, see John Gardner, *On Moral Fiction* (New York: Basic Books, 1978).

LIFE'S EPISODES: STORY AND ITS FORM IN THE EIGHTEENTH CENTURY

Jerry C. Beasley

THE PROSE fiction published in England during the eighteenth century is an immensely varied body of work, rich in its experiments with form, constantly shifting in its attempts to reflect and interpret a baffling world while increasing its appeal to a growing, changing, but always heterogeneous audience. The careful student of this fiction knows, however, that certain common denominators underlie its disparateness to give it a kind of overall unity — or, perhaps more accurate, a distinctive set of identifying features. Novelists of the period, especially the minor ones, were shamelessly imitative; so that famous works — *Robinson Crusoe, Moll Flanders, Pamela, Tom Jones, Clarissa, Tristram Shandy, The Castle of Otranto, The Man of Feeling*, to name but the most obvious examples — always prompted great activity among writers eager to get into print with new stories that would capitalize on the fame of celebrated models. There are other denominators: the recurrence of the biographical mode, particularly in tales of contemporary criminals and saints; the ceaseless preoccupation with private and familiar life, with its emotional content, and especially with its important personal as well as public themes of courtship, marriage, and the threat posed to both by the realities of parental tyranny and rampant licentiousness; the persistence of the conventions of romance and allegory, though nearly always in a context of adaptation and renewal; the common motif of travel, with all its possibilities of adventure, danger, and discovery — discovery of both the world and the self; the insistently topical, ideological, and didactic qualities of most fiction. The list could go on.

I do not mean to suggest that all eighteenth-century fiction is really somehow alike, the differences from work to work no more than the merest superficialities. I *do* mean to suggest that in the days of its early

21

development the English novel depended for its survival and growth upon a process of self-conscious reciprocity. Gradually the accumulating mass, initially lacking identity as it lacked definition, arranged itself into distinctiveness by the sheer exercise of its own replicative energies; until finally, with the appearance of the works of Walter Scott and Jane Austen (two novelists who were themselves deeply aware of the common denominators of eighteenth-century narrative writing), prose fiction gained not only reputation but real status as a species of literature best understood in terms of the mutuality as well as the multiplicity of its formal and thematic attributes. The generic identity of the novel, such as it was, emerged as the variety of its forms addressed a common subject matter of familiar people and familiar experience placed in a context of developing and often perplexing historical circumstance.

If it can be granted that eighteenth-century English novels shared with one another in the several ways I have suggested, then it follows inescapably that their authors looked at the world from a common vantage point which, while certainly broad enough to allow for significantly varied and changing perceptions, nevertheless provided some boundaries to the range of their vision and to the structures and meanings of their narratives. What I shall do in the following pages is focus on a particular feature of earlier fiction — namely, its typically episodic form — that has been frequently noticed by critics and literary historians but never adequately understood as a reflection of one of the truly central ideas governing the pioneering writers who so regularly employed it.[1] My purpose is not simply to elaborate the commonplace that much eighteenth-century fiction is episodic. Rather, I wish to raise, and then try to answer, several different but closely related questions. First, and most broadly, why did writers of popular narratives, from Bunyan to Godwin, so consistently represent life as disjointed, fragmented, resistant to all yearning for order and regularity? More particularly, what influences converged to help determine their way of seeing, shaping, and interpreting experience? What does this background reveal that might help us to become better readers of the fiction itself, better students and critics of the art of early narrative? As I develop my answers to these questions, I hope to suggest some of the ways in which representative individual novels confirm, over time and across formal boundaries, both the preoccupation of their authors with the significance of episodic design and the appropriateness of such design for the audience to which they wrote.

English culture in the late seventeenth century, and throughout the eighteenth century, suffered continual upheaval in every important dimension — economic, social, domestic, political, religious, literary.

Rapidly increasing prosperity in mercantile life, accompanied by the accelerating development of a British commercial and colonial empire, could not mask the reality of new class tensions, of disturbances in the traditional patriarchal structure of the family, of bitter theological controversy and the breakdown of the hegemony of the Church, of increasing democratization of political philosophy, of continuing revolutionary rumblings from the Jacobite adherents of the deposed Stuarts. Grinding poverty and the rampant crime it promoted made the streets of English cities, especially London, dangerous as well as crowded, noisy, and in many areas unspeakably squalid. Brutal press gangs roamed the waterfronts capturing recruits for commercial and military vessels, their methods striking dread into the hearts of young men. There was incessant motion. The rich traveled for their pleasure, from country seat to city to Continent and back again; meanwhile the rural poor migrated in increasing numbers to urban centers, forced into dislocation by agricultural reform and, near the end of the century, by accelerating industrialization.[2]

To modern eyes it may appear that the Enlightenment brought with it liberation from the unhappy confinements of tradition. Those who lived through the period, and many of those who wrote about living through it, saw it in a different way. Lacking the comfort of a name for all that they observed and felt, they could only wonder, resist, or try to understand. Writers like Swift and Pope, in satires addressed directly to the facts of what they believed to be progressive corruptions in taste, politics, and public morality, raged at or scorned the winds of change. Anyone who has read *Gulliver's Travels* (1726) and the *Dunciad* (1728) knows that England was not resting easy during the 1720s. A generation after the great angry satires of Swift and Pope, Johnson's *Rasselas* (1759) took a different approach to similar concerns, acknowledging the inevitability of change but subjecting it to cool philosophical analysis in a story of frustrated expectations and defeated desire. Johnson's imaginary world, for all its exotic quaintness and for all its creator's urgent insistence on the relevance of lessons from the past, looks very much like the landscape of a troubled future in which nothing is certain but the folly of human questing after tranquility and happiness. By the end of the eighteenth century two revolutions, both of them followed by traumas and strife in the lands where they took place and in England itself, seemed to confirm Johnson's skepticism. Stability, however necessary to some, seemed no longer possible to many, no longer desirable to others. Even the genius and eloquence of a Burke could not forestall the fervor of the 1790s or obscure the effects of radical writers like Thomas Holcroft, William Godwin, and Mary Wollstonecraft, whose essays and novels attacked all vestiges of tradition in English political, social, and domestic life.

The novelists just mentioned actually exploited their consciousness of change, seeking its acceleration. The structures of their narratives— Holcroft's *Anna St. Ives* (1792), for example, and Godwin's *Caleb Williams* (1794)—achieve coherence by dramatizing upheaval and the fragmentations it causes, leading in Holcroft's work to new stability founded upon a newly perfected order and in Godwin's work to a kind of nihilistic stasis that strangely undermines the revolutionary idealism with which the author began.[3] Other writers of fiction, in earlier years, were no less aware of the remaking of their world, though they were rarely quite so eager to promote the transformation. Indeed, one might argue that a great impetus for the vigorous activity among growing numbers of novelists in the years prior to about 1750 was simply the spreading desire for a literature of immediacy that could confront directly the reality of a fluctuating present while attempting an explanation of it, as many novels did in their stories of familiar characters caught in the midst of a manifestly unstable contemporary environment. Certain works come immediately to mind: Aphra Behn's troubled political fable of *Oroonoko* (1688), along with *Moll Flanders* (1722), *Clarissa* (1747–48), and *Roderick Random* (1748). The heroes and heroines of these early novels, and of many others from the same period, are all subject to external and threatening forces of change. Through the narrative accounts of their lives, their authors seek both to understand and to control those forces through the exercise of the imagination, either dissolving tension by imposing a happy ending upon unhappy experience or, as in *Oroonoko* and *Clarissa*, by dramatizing inevitable destruction and thus condemning the world for its relentless hostility to the individual life.

Ian Watt argues at some length in *The Rise of the Novel* (1957) that early writers of prose fiction shared moral and other essentially extra-literary reasons for their interest in a literature of immediacy, though Watt's real emphasis rests elsewhere, on his concern to discover the sources of an emerging mode of formal realism in fiction.[4] Watt's notion of a formal realism leads inevitably to a paradigm by which some writers must be judged better than others, and so it is finally inadequate to certain larger purposes of historical criticism. But it is extremely relevant, for its helps us to see that Richardson, in a work like *Clarissa*, was developing a novelistic method for anatomizing and evaluating the vexingly uncertain world inhabited by his heroine; and that Defoe, Fielding, and many other writers besides, were experimenting with their own methods, which were not those of Richardson. All of these early novelists contemplate the very real fracturing of experience by the circumstances that give to life its apparent shape — or shapelessness. Hence their characteristically intensive preoccupation with the significance of specific human moments — the episodes of life — as they relate to or help define a larger totality of meaning. And hence also the many different accommodations reached by writers seeking variously to reassure their readers of the permanence of traditional moral values, or to defy the manifest truths about hard temporal experience by referring them hopefully to the redemptive power of a spiritual super-reality, or finally to create new understanding by proposing — as Sterne did — a radically original way of discovering and rendering the elusive ultimate truth about life's scattered details as they sprawl themselves out over time.

The problems faced by early novelists were thus epistemological as well as formal, and it is probably accurate to say of the most serious among them that the desire to find meaning preceded the desire to create appropriate forms. In this they adapted an important tenet of prevailing critical fashion, as stated most influentially by Le Bossu in his *Treatise of the Epick Poem* (1675). The fable, wrote Le Bossu in describing the proper approach to narrative composition, must be ordered according to "the Instruction, and the point of Morality, which is to serve as its Foundation."[5] One suspects that novelists typically proceeded in a manner resembling that prescribed by Le Bossu, but only partially. Fielding no doubt thought of writing a comic-epic-poem in prose when he sat down over *Joseph Andrews* (1742), just as Richardson began *Clarissa* with the idea of making it a Christian prose tragedy. Other novelists had other primary paradigms in view — biography or history, travel narrative, picaresque — as they got underway with their stories. It is equally certain that for most of these makers of new kinds of fictions the act of writing involved a process of discovery through immersion in the confusing welter of real experience as they sought to re-create it imaginatively. By shaping their responses to what they felt and saw, they found both meaning and novelistic form.

In this connection we may usefully recall that Fielding proclaims the newness and appropriateness of the comic-epic form of *Joseph Andrews* in a preface obviously written after the novel itself, while Richardson's defense of *Clarissa* as a new version of tragedy comes in a postscript to the final volume. Smollett, in the mock dedication (to himself) prefixed to *Ferdinand Count Fathom* (1753), developed analogies to painting and to the drama in order to explain the compositional form of his work and, more specifically, to justify its structure as an expansive and "diffused" representation of life in a series of intensive, dramatic verbal pictures.[6] *Ferdinand Count Fathom* followed *Roderick Random* and *Peregrine Pickle* (1751), and the fact that Smollett's first statement of a theory of fictional form was anticipated by three major experiments suggests the degree to which he, like Fielding and Richardson, placed the discovery of meaning before the discovery of appropriate form in the process of artistic creation.

Of course, it is impossible to distinguish the stages of the creative process so clearly as the preceding would suggest. For most early novelists, even those many who probably cared very little about epistemological or artistic issues but worked instead to serve the marketplace by imitating whatever was popular, the relations between meaning and form did not develop in a tidy sequence. Still, it remains true that the vexing nature of observed experience helped to shape the narratives in which it was rendered; and the works of novelists in turn provided readers with imaginative visions of reality often explicitly intended both to demonstrate the actual texture of life and to provide an analogue explaining its immediate or ultimate meaning.

The imaginings of novelists frequently led to searching experiments with eclectic combinations of conventions from popular narrative types. *Tom Jones* (1749) joins history with romance and travel, and *Moll Flanders* merges spiritual autobiography and the criminal life. Early novelists did not hesitate to improvise, which is not to say that they were always reckless about what they were doing. Smollett all but openly acknowledged the improvisational qualities of *Roderick Random*, an erratic adaptation from the picaresque romance that effectively tells a story of mercurial adventures finally brought to a conclusion in equilibrium and joy.[7] When Tristram Shandy declares that he writes the first sentence of his narrative and trusts to God for every other, we know that his author is teasing us with the suggestion that control of form is an artist's illusion, and we also know that the suggestion is at once true and playfully false. Sterne is telling us that, given the chaos of life as it is apprehended in all its swirling minutiae, wholeness and clarity are very difficult to achieve, for the artist as well as for that more ordinary person the reader. The form of *Tristram Shandy* (1759–67) is overtly improvisational and astonishingly experimental. It is decidedly episodic. The telling of the story and the creation of its form appear to occur simultaneously. For Sterne's purpose the form and the illusion of simultaneity are perfect; for they precisely parallel the meaning of the work as an interpretation of the incomplete, fractured life it records.

Tristram Shandy re-creates the perception of experience as a jumble of disjointed episodes in the form of a novelistic argument, while its defiance of the conventions of linear sequencing in narrative suggests an alternative approach to the problem of interpretation. The perception itself was not Sterne's alone; he simply made it overt, using it in the most conspicuous way as a determinant of form and meaning. What Sterne achieved in the structure of *Tristram Shandy*, and what other novelists of his century achieved in the structures of their works, was deeply affected by inheritances from the past. Among the most important of these inheritances were the several narrative traditions—tales of picaroons and other rogues, the comic romance as it developed in response to the popularity of *Don Quixote*, various forms of biographical and autobiographical writing, travel literature—that converged to exert an almost irresistible force upon the eighteenth-century imagination, challenging the old idealism of epic and heroic romance and solidifying the image of the private character thrust into an increasingly familiar context of change and uncertainty. The regularity with which narratives belonging to these traditions developed their plots in patterns of motion and pause reveals that their authors more or less deliberately chose to emphasize the significance of isolated experiences in approaching the larger epistemological problem of defining, or at least describing, a structure of meaning for modern life. Works of all these several kinds continued to appear throughout the eighteenth century, suggesting that their relevance did not soon fade. The traditions themselves, varied as they are in their separate manifestations through particular narratives, may be called paradigmatic in that they directly anticipated and directly reinforced the concerns and the practice of so many of the novelists who inherited them and who, as we have already noted, frequently borrowed from the conventions they established.

The epistemological problem of description and definition that confronted the writers of prose fiction gained additional focus as a result of other forces having little to do—at least initially—with backgrounds in popular narrative. The legacy of puritanism, already much diffused by the middle of the century but still felt in scores of confessional narratives and lowbrow panegyric biographies of Christian heroes, was especially critical.[8] Quite apart from the important fact that the climate engendered by puritanism produced Bunyan's *Pilgrim's Progress*, which everybody read more than any other book except the Bible for above a hundred years after the publication of its two parts in 1678 and 1684, puritan thought promoted a way of interpreting temporal experience in a spiritual context that was peculiarly congenial even to the secular life about which later novelists typically wrote. Much early fiction is, after all, concerned to reconcile the experience of a secular world with a fading but still viable system of sacred values. Certainly this is true of *Robinson Crusoe* (1719), *Tom Jones*, *Clarissa*, and *Roderick Random*, though the urgency of the attempt does not seem so great in such later works as *Tristram Shandy*, *Humphry Clinker* (1771), and *Calob Williams*. The puritan quest to understand the relation between the individual and God quite naturally took a narrative form, usually autobiographical, since the ordinary Christian life—like that of Bunyan's allegorical pilgrim—was understood to be a hopeful progress toward redemption. Originally a subliterary species of exempla addressed to the community of the faithful, puritan narrative gradually became widespread enough in the culture outside to attract the attention of writers like Defoe and Richardson, whose motives were not exclusively private.

The characteristic structure of a puritan autobiography, briefly described, develops in a series of episodes through which the author traces a profoundly solitary passage toward spiritual understanding. The episodic pattern is significant, for repeatedly it is the specific moment that fixes the attention of the self-analytical writer. Thomas Shepard's *God's Plot*, written just a few years before his death in 1649, may illustrate this typical organization. Shepard grasps almost feverishly at the significance of particular experiences—periods of conflict with community, with family and self; periods spent in prayer to God. He does so because he thinks he may find in them the key to spiritual self-knowledge. His experiences as they occur often seem to sink him to chaos, but they are crucial nonetheless, even though they do not form themselves into any configuration that can be fully understood in temporal terms. Connections finally arise only through retrospective interpretation, which places the particulars of Shepard's remembered past in a larger than temporal frame, that of God's plot for mankind. This is, indeed, the only context that can give them meaning. What Leopold Damrosch, Jr. says of puritan autobiography in general may be applied to Shepard's narrative in particular:

> Puritans tended to stress temporal separateness rather than continuity. For the sake of clarity their attitude may be described in three related ways. First, the moments of experience are separate and disjunct; second, interest focuses more on the ongoing present than on past or future; and third, there is a consistent effort to translate time into eternity, history into myth.[9]

This description applies almost equally well to works like *Robinson Crusoe* and *Roderick Random*, which elaborate individual moments until at last a pattern emerges from the autobiographer's consciousness. It bears likewise, though less directly, on *Tom Jones*, *Clarissa*, *Tristram Shandy*, *Humphry Clinker*, and *The Man of Feeling* (1771), all novels that seek form through confrontation with the separateness of experience, finally discovering meaning in a retrospective paradigm that may be in part mythic (the idea of the rural paradise), in part literary (the comic-epic-poem in prose, the Christian prose tragedy), in part religious (the providential designs of Defoe, Richardson, and Fielding)—or, in Sterne's case, in part psychological. The puritan interpretation of human experience may not have appealed directly to all religious and moral sensibilities, but its expression in autobiographical narratives nonetheless helped to establish a familiar approach to a continuing crisis of dislocation in contemporary life.

The puritan legacy was accompanied into the eighteenth century by another of at least equal importance. With the rise and development of empiricist science and philosophy came a dramatic alteration in the most fundamental principles by which the world might be not only observed, but understood. Novelists, even uncultivated scribblers who probably knew little or nothing of Isaac Newton and René Descartes and who may never have read the works of John Locke, were to a great extent governed in their perceptions by the new empiricism, whose pervasive effects helped to encourage the elaborated particularizing of life that marked the fiction of the early eighteenth century. The subject of these effects and their influence upon novelists is too vast and complex to be treated in any depth here, but we may profitably pause over one or two essential points.[10]

Empiricist thought assumed that human experience of the world came to the individual in a formless rush of sensations, impressions, and memories, and that neither the self nor the world could be understood except through a process of analysis and reflection. Laws of causality, the principles of order in nature, indeed all formal patterns of meaning remained impossible to discover and to state until such a process had been completed. In its most superficial attributes, empiricist thought resembled the puritan principle by which evaluation of particular temporal experience was assumed to lead finally toward recognition and understanding of the wholeness of life. The coincidence is of no small consequence; despite their inherent hostility to one another as systems of thought, puritanism and empiricism were mutually reinforcing. Leopold Damrosch helpfully acknowledges the way in which this coincidence affected at least one novelist when he remarks of Richardson's *Clarissa*, a work profoundly influenced by the tradition of puritan introspection, that its story develops "in accordance with the assumptions of Lockean empiricism." *Clarissa* possesses structure but resists apprehension of that structure, says Damrosch; the reader has to deduce both form and meaning by the isolation and analysis of "significant details" from the "flux of circumstance."[11]

If the puritan looked inward at recollected temporal experience to discover its meaning, the empiricist looked outward upon the world, gathering impressions so that they might at last be formulated into the principles of a coherent design. The implications for new awareness of the inner life were important, as Sterne knew when he made the story of Tristram Shandy a record of the empiricist process only, without ever arriving at its conclusion—or, it appears, ever intending to do so.[12] Sterne was transfixed by the associationist psychology that developed as an outgrowth of Lockean thought, and he was a less confident rationalist than many writers and thinkers of the generation preceding his own. To take but two minor examples: John Kirkby and Simon Berington, the authors of a pair of fictional travel narratives all but explicitly written as empiricist experiments, display the rationalist enterprise at its most extreme.[13] These two works focus upon the power of human reason to deduce, without the benefit of Scripture or other assistance, both the presence of God in the universe and the structure of his divinely ordained design. Kirkby's hero, Automathes, is abandoned as a child on a desert island and grows up having developed a scientist's knowledge of the physical world and a theologian's understanding of the principles of the Christian faith. Berington's Gaudentio di Lucca journeys to a remote African nation whose inhabitants have come to an understanding of natural law and to knowledge of God (or El, as they call Him) by the pursuit of right reason.

Both Automathes and Gaudentio, though they inhabit contrived imaginary worlds, follow a method of observation prescribed by empiricist orthodoxy. This is clearly why they not only survive their confinement in alien places, but emerge triumphant from their experience of those places. Barbara Maria Stafford has described the empiricist method of observation as it was practiced in the writings of numerous eighteenth-century explorers, and her words will serve equally well to characterize the imaginary works by Kirkby and Berington. "An insistent empiricism," says Stafford,

> underlay the explorers' method of perception and saved them from complete bewilderment and inarticulateness in the face of an unedited nature. Armed with a sense-oriented and lucid idiom derived from the burgeoning sciences, they could situate themselves in the world and reason about it. The manifest intention behind descriptions and illustrations was not to transform the visible but to be nonstereotypical, to reproduce for the uninitiated eye the earth's novel, unknown, or undepicted realities.[14]

Writers like Kirkby and Berington set out to interpret as well as to record what their imaginary people encounter. Insistently visual, slow in their movement from elaborated episode to elaborated episode, they allow their characters to accumulate the evidence of observation and to draw inescapable conclusions from it. Like Barbara Stafford's scientific travelers, Automathes and Gaudentio attempt to look *at*, instead of looking over, that which is before them. When the observer gazes upon the observed in this way, says Stafford, the eye is "intently engaged by the aggressive identity of a particular object with respect to which the beholder takes up a position" (p. 40); understanding then follows.

That the empiricist approach to the interpretation of life and experience was inadequate to many human needs as they were perceived in the eighteenth century is beyond dispute. John Wesley initiated the Methodist movement largely because he felt that the spread of rationalist thought among many churchmen had left a wake of spiritual deprivation. In aesthetics, the rising interest in the effects of the sublime led to Gothic fiction, which explored dark regions of the self not easily susceptible to cool analysis.[15] Shaftesbury, Francis Hutcheson, and David Hume, all products of the empiricist movement in philosophy, turned intellectual currents toward the examination of human emotion, or sensibility, as an inescapable fact of the interior life. They may have used the methods of empirical analysis, but their subject matter was more elusive than that approached by the scientist.[16]

These are all commonplaces, and they need no further elaboration here. What is interesting is that novelists for the most part felt the inadequacy of the empiricist method too. Richardson's story of the suffering Clarissa Harlowe adapts an empirical method, as Damrosch suggests; but the novel as a whole becomes something much more than a strictly applied empirical method would permit. Its epistolary form creates an abundance of data, full of conflicts and ambiguities introduced as the letter writers construct their own versions of reality. The obstacles to interpretation placed before the reader increase progressively in magnitude and complexity because every letter is the product of a casuist who not only poses as an observer of events but also has a case to make about his or her role in them. Lovelace is the most complete empiricist among the various correspondents, but he looks perversely and with cynical (and sometimes sinister) detachment upon circumstances he has in fact purposefully helped to create. He takes pride in his creative manipulations, and therefore enjoys believing that he understands and controls their consequences. Anna Howe, meanwhile, responds from a distance to Clarissa's frequently anguished communications, pressing for conciliation and arguing the probability of eventual happiness for her friend if only she will decide to re-create the effects of her suffering into submission before Lovelace's designs, thereby making them honorable. Clarissa's own written accounts of her experience, tortured and partial as they often are, affirm her personal worth, the spiritual value of her resistance, and her moral superiority to all those who bedevil her. The observer and the advocate combine in the character of each letter writer; no character possesses — perhaps no character really desires to possess — a complete version of any event, but each is to some extent self-deluded by private conviction about the meaning of what is first felt and is then, in an exercise of observation through recollection, written down.

The reader who would fully understand Richardson's vast accumulation of the details of his characters' private experience has no real choice but to proceed, in something like the manner of the empirical scientist, by cautious analysis toward deduction of structure and meaning. Any other way lies bewilderment, failure of perception, paralysis. Clarissa herself knows this in the end, and the reader must know it too. But Clarissa also seems to know, though she does not always acknowledge it, that the detachment required for analysis and assimilation is impossible in the midst of experience. Richardson's heroine, even as she preserves her resoluteness and moral superiority through seemingly endless conflict and struggle with her family, with Lovelace, and with herself, is nearly always poised somewhere between clarity and confusion. The reader of her story is usually poised there also. Only on the eve of her death, when in the enclosure of her room she ornaments her coffin with biblical inscriptions and with images suggesting her own frailty and the divine promise of eternal life, does Clarissa finally arrive at full knowledge of the meaning of her short earthly existence. The attentive reader arrives at the same destination simultaneously.

Clarissa's busyness over her coffin, morbid as it may seem at first, signifies her readiness for a "holy dying," to use a phrase made familiar a century earlier by Jeremy Taylor. The emblems she employs — a crowned serpent formed into a ring, a winged hour-glass, an urn, a broken lily — are all recognizably religious, and they are illuminated by texts from Job and the Psalms. And yet Clarissa's care over these emblems and texts involves something more than just self-conducted last rites. She is as concerned about the design of the ornamentation as about its content, shaping it as though it were a poem or a painting. The whole configuration becomes a precise and beautiful rendering of an interpretation of life — of mortal life in general, and of her mortal life in particular — as Clarissa has come to see it in the most profoundly Christian terms. Like the empiricist, but through an exercise of faith rather than merely by a process of rational reflection and analysis, Richardson's heroine has at last given form to the formlessness of her experience in the world; like the puritan autobiographer, but by means of observation as well as introspection, she has placed temporal reality in a redemptive spiritual context of eternity that is finally the only context sufficient to justify her suffering and martyrdom.

This product of Clarissa's moral imagination is the most complete thing she has ever created, and its ultimate effect is to proclaim the power of art to discover, to clarify, and to articulate truth. If hard experience threatens to imprison the self within its individual moments or within the walls of its dim confusions, art can be liberating. Richardson knew this, if only intuitively; other novelists knew it too, which is perhaps a reason why images of imprisonment — and actual episodes set in prisons — figure with such importance in so many of their works. Like science, art depends upon reflection, but unlike science it can reveal and explain what is hidden from the sharpest and most observant eye. The novelist's art, more than any other in the eighteenth century, responded to a paradox in the set of assumptions fostered by rationalist thought, a paradox certainly understood by Locke but not always recognized by others in the scientific and intellectual communities. The zeal to isolate phenomena, to respond to them with the intelligence through the medium of the senses, and finally to see them in patterns of wholeness had the effect of encouraging fragmentation of perception, dislocation of sensibilities, and introspection. We have already seen that other developments — literary, social, political, and theological — provided similar encouragement in a similar direction. These developments are all part of one fabric of history, whose strands may not be separated without falsification, except — perhaps — for the purposes of a discussion like this one. Writers of prose fiction reacted to the entire fabric, in narrative forms that paralleled the structure of life itself; and it may even be said that the novel, as an emerging art form, seems to have thrived because it managed both to provide close representation of the broken pieces of objective and subjective experience, as they were scattered by circumstance, and to put those pieces back together again in configurations accessible — but not always easily — to the imagination of readers.

Clarissa, in creating its configuration of meaning, purposefully makes it hard for anyone to discover what that configuration reveals. Fielding places equally heavy demands on the reader of *Tom Jones*, though the conspicuous artifice and the overtly providential design of that novel do announce from the beginning a superstructure of implied significance. In enforcing the reader's sense of that superstructure, Fielding makes a virtue of episodic design, declaring in the introductory chapter to Book II of *Tom Jones* that he will not imitate the "painful and voluminous Historian, who to preserve the Regularity of his Series thinks himself obliged to fill up as much Paper with the Detail of Months and Years in which nothing remarkable happened, as he employs upon those notable

Æras when the greatest Scenes have been transacted on the human
Stage."[17] This is an unjust reference to *Clarissa*, whose supposed "regularity" disguises its own episodic method; but Fielding capitalizes on the
injustice in defending his more selective procedure. "When any extraordinary Scene presents itself," he says,

> we shall spare no Pains nor Paper to open it at large to our Reader; but if
> whole Years should pass without producing any thing worthy his Notice, we
> shall not be afraid of a Chasm in our History; but shall hasten on to Matters
> of Consequence, and leave such Periods of Time totally unobserved. (p.
> 76).

Fielding's use of episodic design actually involves much greater complexity than his playfulness here suggests. In a recent book on *Tom Jones*,
Anthony J. Hassall has demonstrated convincingly that the novel
engages in a dialectic strategy requiring of the reader an unwavering
attention to the often ambiguous and contradictory details of plot, incident, and character, so that by a complicated process of analysis and
assimilation the pattern of meaning so often hinted at by the narrator
may be finally discovered in full.[18] Digressions, ironic misdirections,
and playful tricks regularly defeat attempts to meet Fielding's own
requirement, placing the reader into a precariousness mirroring that of
Tom and Sophia while objectively paralleling the manifest frustrations of
real as opposed to imaginary experience; but the requirement remains.

Defoe, Smollett, Sterne, Mackenzie, and later William Godwin and
Ann Radcliffe all make comparable demands, though in various ways
and in differing degrees of complication. *Moll Flanders* adapts a biographical mode, but without the organizing principles we have since
learned to associate with biographical writing. As he did in other works,
Defoe simply allowed his narrative to create the illusion that it repro-
duced the structure of life itself as his fictional autobiographer understood it, without the mediation of the artist.[19] The result was a straight-
forwardly sequential progression of seemingly random incidents that has
always troubled those readers who go to a literary text with a predisposition to discover some subtle but predictable aesthetic design in it. *Moll
Flanders* resists such a predisposition until the end, concentrating instead
on the accumulation of experience by a movement from stage to stage,
moment to moment, of the heroine's adventures. Defoe was the master
of "the brilliant episode," says Ian Watt, who then goes on to declare that
this genius of early fiction either did not know of or did not care about
the principles of narrative coherence.[20] Without denying the occasional
clumsiness of *Moll Flanders*, one may plausibly argue that the form of this

novel is entirely what its author wanted it to be, that it accords precisely with his artistic and moral aims. Moll fully grasps the meaning of the frantic episodes of her life only when her career in whoredom and criminality is drawing to a close and she finds herself hellishly surrounded by the walls of Newgate prison. If the reader has failed in moral attention to the particulars of Moll's experience as recorded to that point, then sharing in her discovery of new self-knowledge will be impossible — which may help to explain the difficulty so many have had in accepting her conversion and withdrawal from scenes of action.

Many readers have had similar troubles with Smollett's *Roderick Random*, which concludes as the hero at last recognizes the role of "Mysterious Providence" in both the erratic shaping and the ordered resolution of the mercurial pattern of his life.[21] For Moll and for Roderick, as for Tristram Shandy, the process of recollection and narration is a process of analysis leading to knowledge. Mackenzie, in *The Man of Feeling*, takes a different approach to narrative form and to the establishment of its meaning. He drowns his reader in a sea of emotion as he takes the sentimental hero Harley through an erratic series of bitter encounters with a world so hostile as to leave him with nothing to do in the end except what he finally knows he must, which is to die. Mackenzie's design includes the presence of a third-person narrator who draws progressively closer to the central events of the story, forcing the reader into a dual stance: on the one hand a complete and absorbed affection for Harley promoting resistance to the manifest inevitability of his sad end; on the other hand, and finally, a close identification with him leading to full acceptance — with the narrator — of the appropriateness of his death. The world is a "scene of dissimulation, of restraint, of disappointment," Harley says as he breathes his last. "I leave it to enter on that state, which, I have learned to believe, is replete with the genuine happiness attendant upon virtue."[22] The reader achieves full understanding not at this point but later, and simultaneously with the narrator. During the graveside scene of Mackenzie's closing chapter, we are reminded of how, upon passing the same place one earlier day, Harley had "looked wistfully" at the tree that stood there spreading its shade. "There was something predictive in his look!" the narrator recalls; and he concludes ambivalently that the site of Harley's grave perhaps ought to make him hate the world, but cannot: "No," he says, "there is such an air of gentleness around, that I can hate nothing; but, as to the world — I pity the men of it" (pp. 132–33).

In *Caleb Williams*, Godwin creates such initial ambiguity through manipulation of the identification between his ordinary, suffering hero and his reader that balanced interpretation seems impossible. Caleb begins his moral life as a cold rationalist; he ends it in the knowledge that both his will and identity have been crushed. The reader is forced to live Caleb's experience with him as he struggles to re-create it and thereby comprehend it. "My life has for several years been a theatre of calamity," he begins;[23] his narrative account of the life he has lived employs him in collecting the "scattered incidents" (pp. 136–37) of a progression from apparent order and tranquility, into hurried motion and the terrors of uncertainty, and finally into devastating personal collapse. Caleb's memory fixes upon specific events with agonized clarity—for example, the moment early in the second volume when, filled with suspicion as fire almost engulfs the house, he ventures into Falkland's private apartment and discovers the trunk containing the secrets he has been seeking, only to be suddenly interrupted by his enraged master and threatened with murder; or, later, the afternoon when the fleeing Caleb and Falkland arrive almost simultaneously at the inn where Mr. Forester, Falkland's elder brother, has also stopped. Gradually, subtly, such episodes form themselves into a pattern. What frequently appears at first to be coincidence proves not to be that at all, but the relentless development of a law of inevitability evoked by Caleb's own "ungoverned curiosity" (p. 153) about Falkland's hidden past. The incidents of Caleb's life, "scattered" as they truly are, follow destructively one upon another with an insistency he is powerless to diminish or escape, despite all the active energy he invests in his attempts to do so.

Godwin accepted and met an unusual novelistic challenge when he imagined a design so completely merging episodic plot structure with study of the interior life of a character engaged in a process of disintegration. His ingenious achievement in *Caleb Williams* represents a striking and perhaps deliberate inversion of the providential designs of earlier writers of episodic narrative—particularly Fielding, whose sometimes darkly comic study of the criminal life, *Jonathan Wild* (1743), Caleb mentions in a conspicuously ironic way during an early conversation intended to provoke Falkland into self-revelation.[24] The story of Caleb's disintegration offers no promise or hope of redemption. Precisely detailed, it alternately shocks, pains, and perplexes, trapping the reader by the method of its individualized, highly subjective, and often anguished narration. Caleb's slow, deliberate, obsessive inquiry into the horrible truth about Falkland abruptly turns into a crazy pattern by which the pursuer becomes the pursued while his life is shattered into a frenzied sequence of maddening episodes involving guilt, fear, violence, and imprisonment. Faithful servant and benevolent master annihilate one another in a conflict whose ambiguity is deepened by every encounter between them. Where does justice lie? Godwin provides no answer to this question. His narrative is an emblem of the disastrous effects of class tension and oppressive political tradition, and it takes shape as an evolving and powerful representation of historical dislocation, personal alienation, and psychological despair. In the end, there is only nothingness. "I began these memoirs with the idea of vindicating my character," Caleb writes in his concluding paragraph. "I have now no character that I wish to vindicate" (p. 378).

Godwin's contemporary Ann Radcliffe, and other Gothic novelists like Clara Reeve and Sophia Lee, achieve some of the same effects but without the same calculated results. If Godwin overwhelms his reader with repeated episodes of painful psychological and moral ambiguity, Radcliffe calls for more superficial and impressionistic responses to her lavishly detailed Alpine landscapes and to the primal darkness of her castles and subterranean passageways.[25] Her heroes and heroines, usually naive and innocent, are thrust into a gloom that discourages penetration by the light of reason; and the reader, like the characters themselves, is swept away into the imagined alien environment and all but denied the opportunity for reflection and analysis. The understanding thus fails, and indeed it is part of the rhetoric of these novels to cause it to do so. Intensive visual and emotional engagement with the forbidding details of the Gothic world leads to inevitable responses of distress — bewilderment, terror, *angst* — as perception blurs and darkens, and as incident follows incident more deeply into unknown regions of experience. Reason nearly always prevails at last, but only after some violent shock of recognition — such as Emily St. Aubert's discovery that all of the apparently supernatural terrors of the castle of Udolpho had been caused by the human agency of her villainous uncle Montoni — has made accurate, clear-eyed interpretation of events possible.

The lesson of so many Gothic novels is thus a comforting one, though perhaps unintentionally incomplete and contradictory. It relies on a dual notion that rational analysis of life's events is necessary to the survival of sanity and of the self, but that the individual loses the ability to carry out such analysis when confronted by the overwhelming power of emotional experience in response to the unknown. Jane Austen's famous spoof of Gothic fiction, in her delightful treatment of Catherine Morland's fright in the darkened room where she spends her first night at Northanger Abbey, takes full account of the contradictory impulses of works like *The Mysteries of Udolpho*. Austen's mocking assessment of the appeal — both silly and dangerous, in her view — of Gothic fiction leaves criticism nothing to say on the subject. But her assessment hardly does justice to the historical importance of the novels themselves as documents verifying the degree to which developments in eighteenth-century culture had

prepared the way for representations of fragmented experience, psychological alienation, and dualistic physical and emotional landscapes.

Sterne was far more broadly conscious than Jane Austen of the
contradictory — even paradoxical — nature of eighteenth-century life and
of the narrative literature it produced. He was little interested in the
accommodations and reconciliations other novelists insisted upon almost
without exception. Perhaps this is why he still seems so modern. Every
page of *Tristram Shandy* — Sterne calls it, revealingly, "this rhapsodical
work"[26] — sanctifies the individual episode of life, purposely allowing the
perpetual postponement of resolution by triggering other episodes
through memory, thereby defying all expectation of novelistic neatness.
The novel is designed to avoid all usual constraints so as to develop a
new method for representing the individual life in the flux of personal
and historical circumstance.

Tristram Shandy proclaims its originality by openly expressing its
author's scorn for the conventions of sequential design in narrative, and
it repudiates the progressive ordering and closure upon which such a
design usually depends. In the twentieth chapter of the first volume of
his *Life*, Tristram launches playfully but seriously into a defense of his
own (that is, of his author's) method that is also a direct hit at writers like
Richardson and Fielding, and at their readers as well:

> It is a terrible misfortune for this same book of mine, but more so to the
> Republick of Letters . . . that this self-same vile pruriency for fresh adven-
> tures in all things, has got so strongly into our habit and humours, — and so
> wholly intent are we upon satisfying the impatience of our concupiscence
> that way, — that nothing but the gross and more carnal parts of a composi-
> tion will go down: — The subtle hints and sly communications of science fly
> off, like spirits, upwards; — the heavy moral escapes downwards; and both
> the one and the other are as much lost to the world, as if they were still left in
> the bottom of the ink-horn. (pp. 48–49)

Sterne appears to have felt that in his work he was simply more honest
about the real structure of life than his fellow novelists were apt to be. He
does not deny that their apprehension resembles his own — his "composition" has its "gross and carnal parts" too, in the raw facts of its incidents;
but he does deny that their narrative procedures and their apparent
impositions of arbitrary structure are true.[27] The judgment is not fair,
but that is beside the point here. What Sterne reveals is his own extrem-
ity in the matter of episodic design, which suggests both his departures
from and his common cause with the other novelists of his period. His
way of seeing, radical as it is, illuminates the way taken by his
contemporaries.

Ways of seeing, of course, had everything to do with the means by which novelists structured experience, and it is worth the risk of a Shandean digression to pause and reflect upon yet one more ingredient of eighteenth-century culture as an aid to understanding the textures of its novels. The age was visual, and its visual modes were specific. Historical paintings, often grand and idealistic in conception, celebrated great moments of the distant and recent past. Portraiture reached new heights of achievement in the works of Sir Joshua Reynolds, who joined the stately style of European art with the techniques of reproducing a naturalistic likeness. Much more important to the student of the period's fiction than either Reynolds or the historical painters is William Hogarth, whose dramatic studies of familiar life (Hogarth thought of himself as a "dramatic" painter) certainly had a direct effect on important novelists, including Fielding, Smollett, and Sterne. Fielding openly praised Hogarth in the preface to *Joseph Andrews*, and he frequently referred his own character portraits to figures Hogarth had drawn.[28] We have already noted that Smollett, in his mock dedication to *Ferdinand Count Fathom*, undertook to define the form in which he wrote by introducing an analogy of painting. The novel, he declared, is properly a "large diffused picture" comprehending the characters of life as "disposed in different groupes, and exhibited in various attitudes."[29] Here and elsewhere Smollett suggests his indebtedness to the Hogarthian style both for a way of structuring his imaginary worlds and for an approach to character portraiture.

The most obvious connection between Hogarth and mid-century novelists is through the latter's representations of eccentrics and grotesques — Mrs. Jewkes in *Pamela*, Mrs. Slipslop and Beau Didapper in *Joseph Andrews*, Captain Weazel in *Roderick Random* and Lieutenant Lismahago in *Humphry Clinker*, Corporal Trim and Dr. Slop in *Tristram Shandy*. Any one of these figures, and hundreds of others besides, would be completely at home in a Hogarth painting.[30] But there is a more important and subtle connection. Hogarth was a creator of episodic narratives. In *A Harlot's Progress* (1732), *A Rake's Progress* (1733-35), *Industry and Idleness* (1747), *The Four Stages of Cruelty* (1751), and in other series, he designed structures of individual pictures in sequence, each picture precisely and densely detailed, the wholeness of meaning emerging in every completed sequence from the juxtaposition of all the separate parts. The movement from picture to picture typically invokes laws of relentless inevitability. Rakewell is a bad man who predictably ends his career in a madhouse, surrounded by grim images of squalor, degradation, and death. Tom Nero, whose innate viciousness leads him in successive scenes from the abuse of animals to thievery and finally to the murder of a pregnant young woman, earns a most appropriate "Reward" for his cruelty: executed as a criminal and then stretched out dead on a table in the theater of the Barber-Surgeons' Company, he is disembowelled in the interest of medical research as a fascinated crowd looks on. Fittingly, a dog licks his heart, which has fallen on to the floor.[31]

One might argue that in many of Hogarth's series, a law of causality is the ordering principle. Not every novelist who admired his work and felt his influence subscribed to this principle in the same degree, and certainly not Sterne, as we have already seen. Perhaps the early Smollett did; the protagonists of his first three novels — Roderick Random, Peregrine Pickle, and Ferdinand Count Fathom — all suffer deserved consequences of their failings and villainies before they are finally redeemed. Fielding allows Tom Jones to run in a similar course, though the comic distancing promoted by the voice of his ironic narrator creates differing effects. More important than any of this is the way in which novelists paralleled Hogarth's manner of isolating the particular moment as having significance in itself, with or without reference to a larger narrative frame. In a Hogarth series, it is only when the significance of *each* moment has been recognized and assimilated that the whole can be interpreted. The busy visual texture of a Hogarth picture parallels the busy verbal texture of a pictured episode by Fielding or Smollett, whose novels — and especially Smollett's — develop their structures cumulatively, as Hogarth's painterly narratives do.

Richardson's visual method is different, for he tends to show character profoundly isolated both by momentary circumstances and in space; but he is just as intense, just as concerned with the vibrancy of experience in its recollected form, and his pictures have dense and active texture. To be convinced that this is so one need only look again at the great pen-knife episode of *Clarissa* showing the heroine, alone in a small room with the threatening Lovelace, as she declares her intention to kill herself. Richardson's structures, too, differ from Hogarth's; they are slow, massive, sometimes blurred in the outlines of their formation. But they are just as dependent on cumulative effect; and while Richardson's strategy of accumulation may derive more from the traditions of puritan narrative and letter fiction than from Hogarthian pictorial narrative, the comparison is still striking.

Hogarth certainly was not a scientific observer; he responded to his scenes with his emotions as much as with his intellect or his powers of reason. He was an imaginative interpreter of what he saw as well as its empirical analyst. Like the scientist, he looked *at* the world and not over it, but one is tempted to say that he actually looked at and then *through* the world to its centers of truth. His scenes throb with animation; his human figures (as Fielding observed in the preface to *Joseph Andrews*) appear not only to breathe but to think, which suggests that each possesses precisely the interior life dramatized by his or her posture, gestures, bodily shape, and facial characteristics. Each figure is a type, and yet each has an aggressive individual identity that is defined in part by the surrounding details of an entire picture and by the circumstances it represents. As an episodic narrativist, Hogarth was very much in the mainstream of the storyteller's art as it was practiced in his period. His relations with other narrative artists, and especially with novelists, were of course mutual and reciprocal; he affected them, they no doubt influenced him. But the question of influence is not at issue here. What needs emphasis once again, and what the example of Hogarth helps to clarify, is the fact that the makers of narrative in the eighteenth century most typically confronted real experience by acknowledging its apparent fragmentation and lack of structure and then re-forming it into new artistic shapes of their own.

All modern novels, including those written and published during the long period dominated by Defoe, Richardson, Fielding, Smollett, and Sterne, are in some degree episodic. Indeed, it is the preoccupation with individual character as fixed by specific circumstance, trapped by troublesome or threatening events, struggling against isolation and headed for equilibrium or collapse, that distinguishes modern novelistic fiction from older species of elaborated narrative fantasy. One cannot imagine the *Orlando Furioso* of Ariosto, or Spenser's *Faerie Queene*, or Sidney's *Arcadia* written in novelistic form. These works are episodic too, and in the eighteenth century at least Fielding knew the value of what they and other romances like them could contribute to his own very different kind of narrative writing.[32] But Ariosto, Spenser, and Sidney all project nostalgic, idealized versions of remembered worlds that never existed, and they avoid confrontation with the palpable uncertainties of real experience.

It is thus not the program or the ideology or the structure of traditional romance that makes it impossible to conceive the form in novelistic terms, but its fancied vision of transcendent regions of experience that no Robinson Crusoe or Tristram Shandy or Caleb Williams could ever inhabit. Richardson may have borrowed the Christian name of his first heroine from Sidney, but Pamela Andrews could not have lived in the world of the *Arcadia*. We know that the imaginary characters of Defoe, Sterne, Richardson, and Godwin could have lived in the eighteenth century, that many people more or less like them did live then and have lived since. Their literary descendants populate countless novels of the nineteenth and twentieth centuries. They are the inventions of a changing world, the expressions of a troubled sensibility that has depended in part upon its narrative art to place life's episodes on display and to promote meaningful response to their seemingly patternless disjuncture and disorder. The novelists of the eighteenth century learned how to create that display, and they made its creation both a function and a governing principle of their art.

Notes

1 An essay by H. K. Russell, published some years ago, is one of the very few serious critical studies of the subject of early episodic fiction, but its approach is curiously apologetic. Russell distinguishes between what he calls "plotted" and "episodic" novels, as though the latter had no plots; he then goes on to develop at length a claim that even the most radically episodic novels, such as *Moll Flanders*, *Roderick Random*, and *Tristram Shandy*, have a coherence that parallels "to some extent" the structure of a plot. See "Unity in Eighteenth-Century Episodic Novels," in *Quick Springs of Sense: Studies in the Eighteenth Century*, ed. Larry S. Champion (Athens: University of Georgia Press, 1974), pp. 183–96.

2 Derek Jarrett, in the opening chapter of his *England in the Age of Hogarth* (London: Hart-Davis, MacGibbon, 1974), provides a detailed picture of the restless movement characterizing English life at the time, together with a succinct and clear account of the multiple reasons for it.

3 *Caleb Williams* has sometimes been read as a fictionalizing of the principles Godwin had elaborated just one year earlier in his *Enquiry Concerning Political Justice* (1793); but since *Political Justice* is as idealistic as it is revolutionary, arguing the perfectibility of man in an ongoing political process, it seems more appropriate to read *Caleb Williams* as a contemplation of the possible human failure of both idealism and the revolutionary movement. On this point the full title of Godwin's novel is teasingly revealing. It is: *The Adventures of Caleb Williams, or Things As They Are.*

4 The complete title of Watt's book is *The Rise of the Novel: Studies in Defoe, Richardson and Fielding* (London: Chatto and Windus, 1957).

5 Abbé Le Bossu, *Treatise of the Epick Poem* (Gainesville, Fla.: Scholars' Facsimiles and Reprints, 1970), p. 15.

6 Smollett's reference to the drama as a source for his idea of narrative structure is not surprising; like many other early novelists, including Behn, Fielding, and Goldsmith, he wrote plays as well as fiction. No doubt the drama contributed something to the typically episodic pattern of Smollett's novels; more important, it certainly must have taught him—as it taught others—much of what he knew about the strategies for creating scenes and writing dialogue.

7 In June of 1748, just a few months after the publication of his novel,

Smollett wrote to his friend Alexander Carlyle explaining that the entire work was "begun and finished in the Compass of Eight months, during which time several Intervals happened of one, two, three and four Weeks, wherein I did not set pen to paper, so that a little Incorrectness may be excused." See *The Letters of Tobias Smollett*, ed. Lewis M. Knapp (Oxford: Clarendon Press, 1970), p. 8.

8 During the first half of the eighteenth century about one in every ten biographical narratives, both genuine and feigned, treated the life of some contemporary saintly hero or heroine. I have discussed a number of these exemplary works elsewhere, in *Novels of the 1740s* (Athens: University of Georgia Press, 1982), pp. 126–34.

9 *God's Plot & Man's Stories: Studies in the Fictional Imagination from Milton to Fielding* (Chicago: University of Chicago Press, 1985), p. 60.

10 The most important early statement of the principles of empiricist thought was Locke's *Essay Concerning Human Understanding* (1690). For extended, comprehensive discussion of Locke's influence as it was felt by several generations of writers, see Kenneth MacLean, *John Locke and English Literature of the Eighteenth Century* (New Haven, Conn.: Yale University Press, 1936).

11 *God's Plot & Man's Stories*, p. 259.

12 This is not to suggest that Sterne never came to regard *Tristram Shandy* as a finished work. Certainly he did, but it is nevertheless a narrative structure without a familiar or conventional resolution.

13 Kirkby's work, published in 1745, is suggestively entitled *The Capacity and Extent of the Human Understanding*. Berington called his book *The Adventures of Sigr. Gaudentio di Lucca* when it first appeared in 1737, but in a second edition of 1748 the title was changed from *Adventures* to the more explicitly biographical *Memoirs*. Kirkby, incidentally, was Edward Gibbon's tutor; Berington was an admirer of George Berkeley, the distinguished rationalist philosopher and theologian, and for years his story of Gaudentio di Lucca was thought to be the work of Bishop Berkeley.

14 *Voyage into Substance: Art, Science, Nature, and the Illustrated Travel Account, 1760–1840* (Cambridge, Mass.: MIT Press, 1984), p. 40.

15 Edmund Burke's *A Philosophical Enquiry into the Origin of Our Ideas of the Sublime and Beautiful* (1757) was the major seminal document in the development of an aesthetic of the sublime, but many of the ideas Burke elaborated had been circulating for years. See Samuel Holt Monk, *The Sublime: A Study of the Critical Theories in XVIII-Century England* (New York: Modern Language Association of America, 1935).

16 Shaftesbury, in the *Characteristics of Men, Manners, Opinions, and Times* (1711; 1713), adapted the empiricist system to moral philosophy, arguing for an internal moral sense by which the individual might harmonize life with a universal moral order discernible to reason. Hutcheson followed Shaftesbury's lead in several works, perhaps most notably in *An Inquiry into the Original of Our Ideas of Beauty and Virtue* (1725); and Hume, in his *Treatise of*

Human Nature (1739–40), moved from rationalist premises to a consideration of the powers of the imagination.

17 *The History of Tom Jones, A Foundling*, ed. Martin C. Battestin (Middletown, Conn.: Wesleyan University Press, 1975), p. 75.

18 *Henry Fielding's "Tom Jones"* (Sydney, Australia: Sydney University Press, 1979), pp. 74–75.

19 Defoe underscored the importance of this illusion when, in the preface to *Moll Flanders*, he claimed to have done no more as editor than polish up his heroine's rough narrative, recasting it in more modest and therefore more proper words.

20 *The Rise of the Novel*, pp. 130–34.

21 *The Adventures of Roderick Random*, ed. Paul-Gabriel Boucé (Oxford: Oxford University Press, 1979), p. 413.

22 *The Man of Feeling*, ed. Brian Vickers (Oxford: Oxford University Press, 1967), p. 128.

23 *The Adventures of Caleb Williams*, ed. George Sherburn (New York: Holt, Rinehart and Winston, 1960), p. 3.

24 The conversation occurs in the first chapter of the second volume. Caleb also mentions *Tom Jones*, suggesting that Godwin may have been purpose-fully hinting at the significance of his own novel as a revisionist treatment of human character and of human experience in a world vastly different from what Fielding believed it to be.

25 Radcliffe's most popular tales of darkness and terror were *A Sicilian Romance* (1790), *The Romance of the Forest* (1791), and *The Mysteries of Udolpho* (1794). Clara Reeve, in *The Champion of Virtue: A Gothic Story* (1777; reissued as *The Old English Baron*, 1778), and Sophia Lee, in *The Recess* (1783–85), were among the many who anticipated Radcliffe's success. The market for fiction in the 1790s was largely dominated by the Gothic romance.

26 *The Life and Opinions of Tristram Shandy, Gentleman*, ed. Ian Campbell Ross (Oxford: Oxford University Press, 1983), p. 31.

27 It is not clear how attentively Sterne, whose nearest kindred spirit in the eighteenth century was probably Swift, had actually read the works of Defoe, Richardson, Fielding, and Smollett. But he could hardly have escaped awareness of their continued popularity, and thus he must have been conscious of their example. *Tristram Shandy* may not be quite the "anti-novel" it has sometimes been taken for; still, there can be no doubt that it is in part a reaction to what its recent predecessors had established. For one argument that develops convincingly from this premise, see Howard Anderson, "Answers to the Author of *Clarissa*: Theme and Narrative Technique in *Tom Jones* and *Tristram Shandy*," *Philological Quarterly* 51 (1972): 859–73.

28 For extended discussion of the relations suggested here, see Peter Jan De Voogd, *Henry Fielding and William Hogarth: The Correspondence of the Arts* (Amsterdam: Editions Rodopi, 1981). Robert Etheridge Moore, in *Hogarth's Literary Relationships* (Minneapolis: University of Minnesota Press,

1948), more ambitiously treats the larger subject of Hogarth's broad impact on a variety of eighteenth-century writers, including Fielding.

29 *The Adventures of Ferdinand Count Fathom*, ed. Damian Grant (Oxford: Oxford University Press, 1971), p. 2.

30 It is worth noting here that Hogarth furnished frontispieces for the first and second installments of *Tristram Shandy* (Volumes I–II, III–IV).

31 It was common practice for the bodies of hanged criminals to be turned over by the authorities for dissection by medical practitioners. Hogarth seems to have regarded this practice as barbaric, and he makes Tom Nero's end particularly gruesome by placing it in a context of institutionalized cruelty.

32 See Henry Knight Miller, *Henry Fielding's "Tom Jones" and the Romance Tradition* (Victoria, B.C.: Victoria University Press, 1976). Miller argues persuasively that Fielding, when composing *Tom Jones*, had in mind the models provided by early romancers whose works he admired.

THE NOVEL AND SOCIETY:
THE CASE OF DANIEL DEFOE

John Richetti

GENERALIZING from what he calls "panoramic" passages in Dickens' later novels, Jonathan Arac describes the nineteenth-century novelist as a "commissioned spirit" who surveys society from a commanding height and seeks to render "social motion," to provide thereby "a sense of a coherent social totality, buried but operative, waiting to be diagrammed or dramatized in fiction."[1] At first glance, Arac's analysis seems to fit eighteenth-century novels equally well. Social comprehensiveness, or at least a wide range of social representation, is to some extent one of their distinctive features. And yet a commanding overview with its promise of a hidden totality is not quite what the novels of the period provide. What they are about, if looked at closely with the issue of social totality in mind, is precisely the difficulty of imagining the ultimate social coherence that nineteenth-century novelists take for granted.

In *English Literature in History 1730–80: An Equal, Wide Survey*, John Barrell finds writers in those years "concerned to represent the diversity of English society more fully" than ever before.[2] But with that ambition, Barrell points out, comes an increasing sense of the difficulty, even the impossibility, of achieving a comprehensive view of society, now widely perceived as increasingly, bewilderingly complex and diverse. The main problem, as Barrell sees it, is where to place an observer so that he transcends an encompassing social structure in which individuals are defined by their partial and necessarily self-interested economic and political roles. As the economic structure of society becomes more apparent and the landed interest is revealed as one among several competing factions, even the myth of the gentleman-spectator, disinterested by virtue of the leisure guaranteed by his estate, begins to fade. One solu-

tion, says Barrell, is enacted in Smollett's novels, and he quotes the
definition of a novel in the dedication to *Ferdinand Count Fathom* (1753):

> A Novel is a large diffused picture, comprehending the characters of life,
> disposed in different groups, and exhibited in various attitudes, for the
> purpose of an uniform plan, and general occurrence, to which every indi-
> vidual figure is subservient. But this plan cannot be executed with propri-
> ety, probability or success, without a principal personage to attract the
> attention, unite the incidents, unwind the clue of the labyrinth and at last
> close the scene by virtue of his own importance.[3]

As Barrell points out, the novel's hero, the "principal personage," adds a
crucial diachronic or historical dimension to the frozen motion of Smollett's crowded picture. It is by virtue of his experience within that diversity, his sampling of a wide variety of its specific possibilities without
ever limiting himself to any particular one, that he is enabled to write the
novel, that is, to become a gentleman-autobiographer and achieve both
knowledge and distance, both participation and contemplative perspective. As Barrell observes, such a gentleman is palpably a fiction, possible
only in fiction.[4] But such a solution and such a fictional narrator are
conspicuous by their absence from several of the other major eighteenth-
century novelists.

In Defoe, Richardson and Fielding's works, the eighteenth-century
novel features an enormous diversity of social representation, and individual books present a varied canvas, rather like one of those exuber-
antly crowded scenes from Hogarth in which the viewer is teased to find
a center or principle of order, in which comic chaos seems a deliberate
parody of orderly plenitude. That same ambiguity Hogarth depicted
seems to operate in eighteenth-century fiction, for in their different
ways, the novelists pretend to cede authority in the search for a center,
deferring to characters or fictional narrators to make whatever sense
they can of social diversity. Such deferral, for example, is part of the
function of Fielding's ironically self-depreciating narrative stance in
Joseph Andrews and *Tom Jones*, and the patterns of comic romance that
resolve both of those books are in this sense a declaration that social
actuality admits of no clear or self-evident ordering principle. Perhaps,
Fielding clearly implies, there is an analogy between his resolving intervention in the plot of *Tom Jones* and the operations of Providence in the
universe. But the mysterious coherence of the universe and the comic
novel that mimics it stand out against the incoherence of human society,
whose disorder serves as the material screen for the hidden cosmic
design. So, too, Richardson's coy invisibility behind his characters' let-

ters and, in *Clarissa* at least, his appeal from the legal complications and socio-economic entanglements of the plot to the heroine's Christian transcendence and transfiguration are strategies for avoiding any sort of social synthesis. Implicitly, it is only the novelist who has any *actual* claim to a comprehensive view of society, but that claim is invariably indirect or ironically deferred. Put this diffidence next to the powerful synthesizing vision of the nineteenth-century novelists Arac speaks of, and the contrast is striking.

However, this crucial difference between narratives from the two centuries should not surprise us, since, in a strict sense, "society" as the totality Arac invokes did not fully exist for the eighteenth century. As Raymond Williams concludes in *Keywords: A Vocabulary of Culture and Society*, the word has come to signify in the most *general* sense possible "the body of institutions and relationships within which a relatively large group of people live" and in the most *abstract* sense "the conditions in which such institutions and relationships are formed." But as Williams shows, those meanings were not prevalent in England until the last third or so of the eighteenth century. Till then the older associations of the word prevailed: from Latin *socius* = companion, and *societas* = companionship and fellowship. Society signified something active and immediate, not an institutionalized totality but a decidedly smaller and specifically connected group of people.[5] That usage can be accounted for by borrowing some terms from the social theorist, Anthony Giddens. Britain in the eighteenth century is not yet a modern nation-state but rather a "class-divided" society in which large spheres "retain their independent character in spite of the rise of the state apparatus."[6] In Giddens' evocation of them, class-divided societies display a "segmental character" that resists the centralized administration characteristic of the modern state. But as he suggestively charts its accelerated development in the eighteenth century, that state clearly emerges as writing becomes more and more "a means of coding information, which can be used to expand the range of administrative control exercised by a state apparatus over both objects and persons."[7]

From this very broad cultural perspective, the eighteenth-century novel can be said to form part of an emerging social formation, connected at the least as a parallel phenomenon to an increasingly efficient ordering of objects and persons through written documents and records, as the organized totality called the nation-state begins to materialize. Paradoxically, the intensely individualistic ordering drive of novelistic narration can easily turn readers toward the rationalized bureaucratic norms just then beginning to emerge. In eighteenth-century narrative, it can be argued, historically specific individuals begin to emerge with a new clarity and insistence. Such figures are elaborately, pointedly derived from local and particularized social and historical circumstances rather than from the generalized moral essentialism of literary tradition. Implicitly, the novel as a new narrative mode argues for rationalized social arrangements that can respond to the needs of these unique or at least unpredictably individualized characters, who tend to be presented as such rather than as part of a traditional system of predetermined roles and functions in which understanding the repetition of perennial patterns is the key to moral and social knowledge.[8]

But as they appear in eighteenth-century narrative, these newly distinctive individuals and their surrounding and determining social circumstances lack the clear-cut separation or even opposition that is the troubling by-product of modern bureaucratic arrangements. As Alasdair MacIntyre formulates it, the moral history of the last two centuries has made the self a ghostly thing apart from its roles and social locations. Using Sartre and Erving Goffman as ideological opposites, MacIntyre finds that their separation of the self from society comes to the same thing. For Goffman, the self is a nebulous entity until it materializes as a part of social relationships and functions; for Sartre it can authentically appear only apart from those roles and functions.[9] Self and society, in this familiar antithesis, would seem to be the novel's defining thematic opposition: private experience realizes itself as such, whether false or authentic, within and against the surrounding structures of public life or society in the totalizing sense uncovered, sometimes with horror, by the nineteenth-century novelists. Instead of this tense, mutually excluding, and therefore clear and defining opposition between the two terms, the eighteenth-century novelists render various sorts of intersections and infiltrations between them, mutually defining relationships that dramatize an inevitable interdependence or even an inseparability between self and society that tends to nullify the distinction.

"Society" as it appears in eighteenth-century fiction, like the older societies Giddens describes, lacks clearly marked borders. In much of this fiction, characters may be said to move through vaguely defined frontier areas, where domestic and public spaces overlap and where administrative control and definition are loose or ill-defined. Part of Richardson's Pamela's problem, for example, is that her would-be seducer is nothing less than one of the legal representative of the law, the chief landowner and therefore the magistrate in his part of Lincolnshire where he besieges her virtue. Instead of a monolithic and compellingly authoritative social structure, characters in this fiction often encounter a diffuse and diverse collection of individuals only partially defined by the institutional arrangements of which they are a part. Such a society, in

Harold Perkin's influential evocation of it, was linked by the quasi-personal relationships summed up in patronage, a "middle term between feudal homage and capitalist cash nexus." As Perkin puts it, eighteenth-century society consisted of "permanent vertical links," a "durable two-way relationship between patrons and clients."[10] But in the narrative versions of such a society, characters often define themselves by elaborate manipulation of or resistance to just these patronage relationships, which appear invariably as inefficient or corruptly and sometimes comically ineffective. Within the satirical tradition that shapes, for example, Smollett and Fielding's novels, these relationships that historians tell us were the social actuality are comically riddled by the force of a moral essentialism or universalism whereby individual corruption and self-seeking are built into all larger social arrangements. Comic moralism is nothing less than an awareness of the eternal recurrence of thinly disguised moral deviance from social values or the manipulation for profit and advantage of institutions by individuals. Such comedy is implicitly conservative, since there is no escaping the eternally human. Social structures are comically factitious; they have in the end no real effect or determining power to alter human nature.

And yet for all the force of that tradition and for all the emotional investment characters and narrators have in moral and religious transcendence, these novels are crowded with many fragments of contemporary actuality and point in certain reformist directions at particular institutions such as the armed forces and the clergy, the game and the debt laws, and the justice system in general, and at larger and more generalized social arrangements such as marriage and the family. Except for Richardson, the novelists were polemical and political writers first and novelists only as the literary marketplace led them to it. They balance historical specifics and seemingly intractable social problems against resolving and reassuring moral generality. In fact and in practice, society and social relationships in general present themselves in the novels especially of Fielding and Smollett as a sort of improvised absurdity, fragmentary and unsystematic precisely because of their historical particularity. Totality and coherence represent moral rather than social possibility.

Of the major novelists of the eighteenth century, Defoe had the most extensive and elaborate views of the social structure of his time, and next to Fielding and Smollett, the depiction of social relationships in his fiction seems more attuned to what look like actualities that resist the recurrent patterns of comic moralism. Perhaps simply because he was less concerned with literary tradition and its accompanying moral universalism, his narratives seem to render or at least imply something like a social totality. As a political journalist and an aggressive expositor to the public of what we now call economics, Defoe took from the very beginning of his career an explicitly totalizing view of society in order to promote practical measures to make it more efficient and, to some extent, more rational. *An Essay on Projects* (1697), his first published book, is concerned with schemes for national improvement, as the subtitle puts it, with "the means by which the subjects in general may be eased and enriched." Although Defoe was not quite the progressive or forward-looking thinker he is sometimes taken for, he does consistently display in his economic and political journalism an ambition to comprehend something like social totality. But his vision was in fact necessarily partial. As Peter Earle points out, Defoe "wrote voluminously on the sections of society which he knew best or whose problems interested him but he never really tried to analyse society as a whole."[11]

But Defoe does have recurring moments of totalizing social vision. His imagination was stirred by what he saw as the grand spectacle of "trade," a socio-economic sublimity visible in the market system's wonderful and mysterious combination of finely calibrated efficiency and sweeping, all-encompassing variety. In *A Brief State of the Inland or Home Trade of England* (1730), he invokes economic process as a reflection of cosmic order and social structure:

> . . . with what admirable skill and dexterity do the proper artists apply to the differing shares or tasks allotted to them, by the nature of their several employments, in forming all the beautiful things which are produced from those differing principles? Through how many hands does every species pass? What a variety of figures do they form? In how many shapes do they appear? — from the brass cannon of 50 to 60 hundred weight, to half an inch of brass wire, called a pin, all equally useful in their place and proportions. On the other hand, how does even the least pin contribute its nameless proportion to the maintenance, profit, and support of every land and every family concerned in those operations, from the copper mine in Africa to the retailer's shop in the country village, however remote?[12]

Defoe's most elaborate and eloquent renditions of this kind of socio-economic totality can be found in *A Tour Thro' the Whole Island of Great Britain* (1724–26), which is punctuated by moments of wonder at the inexhaustible plenitude of modern economic life, with its quantities beyond individual comprehension: the million and a half turkeys driven to London from Suffolk each year, the uncountable number of mackerel caught off the Dorsetshire coast, the hundreds of thousands of sheep sold at the Weyhill fair in Wiltshire, the corn markets at London ("the whole world cannot equal the quantity bought and sold here"), and the seemingly endless lines of ships in the river from London Bridge to Blackwall: "The thing is a kind of infinite, and the parts to be separated from one another in such a description, are so many, that it is hard to know where to begin."[13]

Defoe's various and recurring renderings of this socio-economic totality naturally involve an observer who understands it for what it is by preserving a certain distance from it. Such an overview seems available only to the contemplative outsider, or at least would seem to require the bemused spectatorial posture of the eighteenth-century essayist, a matter in Addison's famous formulation in the *Spectator* of considering the world as a theater, living in the world without having anything to do with it. But in the *Tour* and his other economic journalism, Defoe speaks as a participant, immersed and involved in the vast system he evokes, delivering an insider's first-hand experience as the sustaining pre-condition for those moments of contemplative wonder at the totality.

Defoe's perspective on socio-economic totality thus includes the possibility of meaningful action within it. Precisely within this grand and controlling socio-economic panorama stands the heroic individual who manipulates that totality, preeminently the tradesman, who is in the process of transforming English society and reinvigorating the ruling class. "How are the antient families worn out by time and family misfortunes," he wrote in 1725, "and the estates possess'd by a new race of tradesmen grown up into families of gentry and establish'd by the immense wealth gain'd, as I may say, behind the counter; that is, in the shop, the warehouse and the compting-house? How are the sons of tradesmen rank'd among the prime of the gentry?"[14] And even when the tradesman is defeated by the system, his unfailing energies can bring him to the top again. "No condition," Defoe insists, "is so low or so despicable in a tradesman, but he may with diligence and application recover it." A force of nature, the tradesman "rolls about the world like a snowball, always gathering more, always increasing, till he comes to a magnitude sufficient to exist of himself, and then he boldly shews himself in the same orbit, in which he first shin'd."[15]

Defoe's own experience as a businessman bears out only part of this evocation of the heroic merchant. Bankrupt twice for substantial sums of money, he continued to struggle financially all his life, and in his transformation into a journalist and political operative for opposing factions exemplified the difficult, specifically social relationships he dramatized later in his fiction. That is to say, the comprehensive vision of society Defoe offers in his economic journalism inevitably breaks down in his life and in his fiction, giving way to the experience of particular and personal patron-client relationships in which society appears not as a grand totality but is approached necessarily from within as a set of pressing local problems for the individual. In practice rather than from the enthusiastic generalizing heights of theory, Defoe's vantage point on social experience is internal, partial and pragmatic, an insider's perspective, sometimes subversive and manipulative, sometimes deeply and confusingly implicated. To be sure, the insider's first-hand slant of Defoe's narratives seems to have been dictated by his assessment of the literary marketplace. Pseudo-autobiographies such as he produced in the 1720s were clearly designed to appeal in their immediacy to a wider audience than perhaps more overtly fictional and generalizing third-person narratives would have reached. But as they appear in Defoe's fictions, social relationships are not mastered in the long run by the convention of retrospective contemplative knowledge John Barrell finds implicit in Smollett's novels. Instead of transcending an encompassing social structure, Defoe's fictional autobiographers tend to negate its potentially totalizing force by rendering it from the point of view of their defensive participation within in it as a series of discrete and essentially discontinuous moments without the coherent force of a supervising totality. But, and this I think is the most fascinating aspect of the social vision of Defoe's fiction, some of the novels simultaneously dramatize the irresistible influence of larger social structures and evoke at times a controlling if subterranean totality as the ground of the erratic and improvisational individualism they seem to celebrate.

Let me turn for the rest of this essay to particulars from two of Defoe's narratives, *Moll Flanders* and *Colonel Jack*, that will show how they manage this crucial balance. Put broadly, Defoe's narratives seem to stage an evasion of that social totality I've been discussing, that is, of the determining material conditions of personality and destiny that the books seem to validate by their narrative mode. The documentary surface of these narratives, their self-definition as case histories, ratifies as genuine exceptional individuals, whose extraordinary status in some sense both transcends and verifies those ordinary circumstances from which they spring. The relationship between these spheres of experience presents itself as dynamic, since the "documentary" force of these narratives is to a large extent an effect of the detached freedom of the narrative voice, which also at the same time insists on its location within specific social experience, its derivation as a particular voice from the circumstances it documents.

On the one hand, as Ian Watt reminds us, novels like Defoe's depend upon the value society places on each and every individual so that daily life at its most trivial acquires serious significance.[16] But on the other hand, it can be argued, Defoe's novels dramatize irrelevance and marginality at the heart of individual experience; they argue powerfully as narrative enactments for the inherent insignificance and merely private nature of individual actors, whose claim to our attention is in fact a miraculous survival in the face of an external world that is brutal and normally inescapably confining and determining. His narrators, if we think about them, exist as responses (sometimes inventive ones to be sure) to the stimuli of material circumstances; they are whatever they have to be, whatever circumstances require of them. Intensely present individuals, they are at the same time recurring testimony to a larger reality that produces them or drives them on and makes them of interest.

Of all Defoe's characters, Colonel Jack has the most varied career and the most self-consciousness about the influence of a larger reality on personal destiny. The book's title page sketches crudely the broad historical sweep of his career and makes much of Jack's rise from pickpocket to planter and merchant to gallant officer: *The History and Remarkable Life of The Truly Honourable Col. Jacque commonly call'd Col. Jack, who was born a gentleman, put 'prentice to a pick-pocket, was six and twenty years a thief, and then kidnapp'd to Virginia. Came back a merchant, married four wives . . . went into the wars, behav'd bravely, got preferment, was made Colonel of a regiment, came over, and fled with the Chevalier, and is now abroad compleating a life of wonders, and resolves to dye a General* (1722). Whether Defoe or the bookseller contrived this wide-eyed summary, it is in fact untrue in its simple exuberance to the book's complex evocation of the relationship between private experience and social identity. As many commentators have noted, Defoe renders Jack's early days as a street urchin and then as a teen-age hoodlum with rare psychological sensitivity. He makes Jack a hesitant thief, a sensitive and confused street boy surrounded by cruder, thoughtless comrades. Told by the old woman paid to raise him that he is the bastard son of a gentleman, Jack recalls his sense of his special destiny and singularity, manifest especially in two characteristics: intellectual curiosity and moral sensitivity. "I was always upon the Inquiry, asking Questions of things done in Publick as well as in Private," he remembers, and thus became "a kind of an Historian," illiterate but able to "give a tollerable Account of what had been done, and of what was then a doing in the World."[17]

Later on Jack will participate actively in these fascinating great events, and the moral sensitivity that is his other distinguishing mark as a child will turn out to be instrumental rather than self-expressive, serving in effect to propel him out of his degraded and localized childhood scene and into that great world. For Jack has a "strange kind of uninstructed Conscience" (p.55) that makes him, at least as he remembers it, less than a full participant in the criminal sub-culture in which he grows up. Unlike his mates, he has an awareness at once moral and economic, a reverence for the mysterious documents of the mercantile world that intertwines with his reluctance to hurt others. So he cannot bring himself to destroy the "Bills and Papers" of the merchants whose pockets they pick: "things that would do them a great deal of hurt, and do me no good; and I was so Tormented about it, that I could not rest Night or Day, while I made the People easie, from whom the things were taken" (p.55). Taken before a justice, his "Heart was full of Terror and Guilt" (p.77); hearing that his comrade, Will, is in Newgate, Jack's "very Joints trembl'd" and his "Head run upon nothing but *Newgate*, and the Gallows, and being Hang'd; which I said I deserv'd, if it were for nothing but taking that two and twenty Shillings from the poor old Nurse" (p.75). A creature of his richly evoked environment and, like all of Defoe's irrepressibly self-inventing narrators, clever and resourceful at surviving within its possibilities, Jack by means of this intellectual and moral sensitivity dramatizes a confused awareness of a larger network of supervising social institutions.

Jack's defining gesture as a coherent character, then, his distinctive and driving obsessive fear of the gallows, links his interior life with a comprehensive exterior order. Placed at the margins of society, Jack validates its centrality by the intensity of his defensive interior life, by the energy and variety of his attempts to avoid its power, and in the end by his internalization and recapitulation of its organizing principles. To some extent, and paradoxically, Jack acquires a complex self (as opposed to a merely sociological identity as street urchin or the literary role of picaro-adventurer) by articulating a relationship with the comprehensive social structure exemplified in the terrifying penal system.

One incident in Jack's early career can serve to illustrate these relationships. In a scene set in Edinburgh, Colonel Jack looks rather clearly at some peculiar actualities of that penal code. On the run from English law, he and his chum, Captain Jack, survey first the center of the town, "throng'd with an infinite Number of People" (p.99), and then in that mass of people they see "a great Parade or kind of Meeting, like an *Exchange* of Gentlemen, of all Ranks and Qualities" (p.100). Suddenly, the scene grows specific and detailed, the crowd runs to "see some strange Thing just coming along, and strange it was indeed":

for we see two Men naked from the Wast upwards, run by us as swift as the Wind, and we imagin'd nothing, but that it was two Men running a Race for some mighty Wager; on a sudden, we found two long small Ropes or Lines, which hung down at first pull'd strait, and the two Racers stopp'd, and stood still, one close by the other; we could not imagine what this meant, but the Reader may judge at our surprize when we found a Man follow after, who had the ends of both those Lines in his Hands, and who when he came up to them, gave each of them two frightful Lashes with a Wire-whip, or Lash, which he held in the other Hand; and then the two poor naked Wretches run on again to the length of their Line or Tether, where they waited for the like Salutation; and in this manner they Danc'd the length of the whole Street, which is about half a Mile. (p.100)

This man, Jack explains at the end of the episode, "was the City Hangman; who (by the Way) is there an Officer of Note, has a constant Sallary, and is a man of Substance, and not only so, but a most Dexterous Fellow in his Office; and makes a great deal of Money of his Employment" (p.101).

Jack balances fear (or the vivid memory of it) with an exact appreciation of the fitness of institutionalized punishment and admiration here for its official administrator. The anxious immediacy of Jack's connection with the scene of punishment is modified by the appearance in the wake of the pickpockets of the impressive, efficient figure of the City Hangman. Stable power and authority correct what seems to begin as urban confusion and appears at first to be a near riot or spontaneous street happening: two half-naked men and a crowd running after are brought up short and punished soundly by lines of control that were not immediately visible. The two young "Jacks" on the road of picaresque criminal adventure, improvising escape and survival, are like those two pickpockets, running free but actually held by invisible tethers that grow all the more taut as they seem to move away from the law and its punishments. The open road of literary adventure gives way to the orderly and exact rendering of the actual Edinburgh Defoe knew so well from his days as a political operative for Robert Harley. Supervising order, something like a suddenly manifest social totality, transforms the city and aligns its crowded streets into an arena for staging the orderly inevitability of public discipline.

This vivid scene is replayed in Jack's future, first obsessively and overtly as a horrible memory. As he says a bit later on when he enlists in the army: "I had a secret Satisfaction at being now under no Necessity of stealing, and living in fear of a Prison, and of the leash of the Hangman; a thing which from the time I saw it in *Edinborough*, was so terrible to me, that I could not think of it without horror" (p.104). But eventually the scene, along with the implicit model of power and social control it contains, is recapitulated in Jack's own experience, made a part of his own reformation in Maryland, first as an overseer and then as a plantation slave master. Jack understands, as no one else in the plantations does, that the unsystematic cruelty and *ad hoc* suppression of the slaves is inefficient; merely particularized and reactive, such management lacks the calculated purpose and long-range effectiveness of the policy Jack devises. "But I began to see at the same time, that this Brutal temper of the *Negroes* was not rightly manag'd; that they did not take the best course with them, to make them sensible, either of Mercy, or Punishment; and it was Evident to me, that even the worst of those tempers might be brought to a Compliance, without the Lash, or at least without so much of it, as they generally Inflicted" (pp.128–29). Jack, the managerial innovator, is an overseer who develops a mode of punishment for his master's slaves whereby the customary simple brutality is replaced by psychological manipulation: Jack's threats to recalcitrant slaves of terrible punishment are tempered by theatricalized mercy from above, from the "Great Master" Jack serves.

Such terrorizing resembles in its workings the brutal logic behind the penal code as Jack has experienced it, and indeed near the end of his narrative he will benefit from a royal pardon extended to Jacobite rebels. Jack expresses in America what he may be said to have internalized as an untutored and terrified street urchin, an appreciation of the ways in which institutions regulate their members. In Maryland, Jack becomes the perfect exporter of social forms, for he successfully institutionalizes the controlling threat of punishment that has shaped his life. To be sure, there is much more to *Colonel Jack* than this transition from marginalized thief to colonial manager. Jack's subsequent career as Jacobite adventurer and illegal trader in the Spanish Caribbean complicates his personality considerably, and in the somewhat forced variety that makes Jack a soldier in European wars and a much-married man, his career also dissipates the implicit coherence I have outlined.

Moll Flanders (1722) is somewhat less extravagantly varied and more nearly unified in its rendering of an implicit social coherence. Like Jack, Moll negotiates a maze of difficult social conditions, at their most memorable and intensely actual in urban crime and punishment. And like him, she derives her identity from an avoidance of the inevitability built, as she herself assures us, into just those circumstances, transforming by virtue of her efficiently subversive marginality those actualities into opportunities for self-expressive survival and even prosperity. Eventually, Moll's growing fear of the actual penal retribution summed up in Newgate prison links her inner dimension to social externality that seems at first glance to diminish her individuality. But in looking back and evoking her distinctive subjectivity, Moll's narrative renders her obsessive, introspective self-consciousness as in effect a means of separation from that actuality. What Moll insists upon, what she claims was extraordinary in her life and worthy of a reader's attention, is her talent for manipulative impersonation provoked by her singular self-consciousness of an external world that threatens at any moment to negate her as the individual she insists she always was.

From her early days at Colchester, Moll resembles Jack in her self-defining apartness from those around her, but she is more quickly absorbed as an upper servant and mistress and then as a wife into the middle-class family that adopts her. Moll acquires, that is to say, a greater ease than Jack within broadly defined social institutions. She learns rather quickly the tricks of self-preservation and plausible self-invention, and all these feints sustain her in a world where female survival is shown to be difficult. Moll defines herself as someone who learns quickly to analyze social possibility in generalized terms and to situate herself accordingly. Echoing some of Defoe's own remarks on the social situation but quarreling with the conventional sociological wisdom, Moll surveys the sexual field after her second husband leaves her: "They, I observe insult us mightily, with telling us of the Number of Women; that the Wars and the Sea, and Trade, and other Incidents have carried the Men so much away, that there is no Proportion between the Numbers of the Sexes; and therefore the Women have the Disadvantage; but I am far from Granting that the Number of the Women is so great, or the Number of the Men so small."[18] The problem, says Moll, lies rather in the limited number of men "fit for a Woman to venture upon." Moll thus begins her career in society with a cynical sense of the fluidity and indeed the irrelevance of its categories but also with an exact sense of those categories and their importance. Here she is, with all those intellectual features on display, setting out in the world after the death of her first husband: "I was not averse to a Tradesman, but then I would have a Tradesman forsooth, that was something of a Gentleman too; that when my Husband had a mind to carry me to the Court, or to the Play, he might become a Sword, and look as like a Gentleman, as another Man; and not be one that had the mark of his Apron-strings upon his Coat, or the mark of his Hat upon his Perriwig; that should look as if he was set on to his Sword, when his Sword was put on to him, and that carried his Trade in his Countenance" (p.60). Shortly after this, she and the "gentleman-tradesman" she marries go for a romp to Oxford posing as "quality," and in her subsequent career as a female con artist and pickpocket-shoplifter Moll's *modus operandi* lies precisely in various kinds of social impersonation.

However, it is worth noting that Moll makes crucial errors of judgment: not only does her tradesman husband prove feckless, but the Irish gentleman she marries later turns out to be a fortune-hunter and the Virginia planter she marries proves to be no less than her brother. Of course, this last is hardly an error of judgment; Moll seems trapped by an inscrutable, unavoidable pattern of enclosing coincidence. Right next to her exuberant chronicle of self-improvisation within the unpredictable, linear sequentiality of her life is a gathering, circular pattern of fatality and necessity, exemplified by her inadvertent return to her biological family in Virginia, just when she thought she was getting as far away as possible from her origins. So, too, her career as the most successful thief of her day (the "greatest Artist of my time" [p.214]) leads inevitably back to her origins in Newgate. Yet Moll hardly prepares us for that development. In narrating the social relationships that make up her varied life, she ruthlessly renders them in economic terms and shows how she managed them by shrewd sexual liaisons and opportunistic crime. The novel's varied social panorama has its stabilizing center in just that economic analysis, which reduces and particularizes, tracking from crowded social possibility and generality to focus on individual motives and solutions within that larger scene.

In telling her story, Moll may be said to accept the constraints such elaboration reveals, constituting herself as she narrates by retrospectively locating a self within a system of causes, variously social, economic, psychological, and even providential, that point to something like a controlling totality. But the parts do not quite add up to that whole, since these moments of destiny are at one and the same time opportunities for escape and expansion in which experience promotes another, more liberating sort of freedom whereby necessity becomes redefined as imperfectly confining and serving to release hitherto unexplored resources in the self. Yet Defoe seems instinctively to want to dramatize a coherence larger than the sum of Moll's individual transactions, and that underlying unity is present in part through the providential pattern that seems to appear retrospectively as the narrative unfolds. There is a final turn to the screw that evokes something like a social totality. *Moll Flanders* rehearses in a powerfully implicit way the contradiction that the free, intensely unique individual is somehow the result of an exactly rendered and accumulating necessity, a social totality partly obscured by the energy of autobiographical retrospection and only clearly visible, I think, in one crucial sequence.

A few key particulars will illustrate this movement in the narrative, first away from a potentially totalizing understanding of experience in the expression of a developing subjectivity. Consider Moll's seduction by the elder brother in the family at Colchester. Innocent and inexperienced, she is surprised by the desires he arouses in her but even more flustered by the discovery of the powerfully eroticized force of more money than she has ever seen. Young Moll, classless interloper in the upper-middle-class house in Colchester, embodies natural physical gifts, and she speaks in these scenes with her body as the elder brother fires her blood with ardent kisses and declarations: "my heart spoke as plain a voice, that I liked it; nay, whenever he said, 'I am in love with you,' my blushes plainly replied, 'Would you were, sir'" (p.22). After her lover tumbles her on the bed, he gives her five guineas: "I was more confounded with the money than I was before with the love, and began to be so elevated that I scarce knew the ground I stood on" (pp.23–24). Moll can only look back and wonder at her own inability then to "think," for she "thought of nothing, but the fine Words, and the Gold" (p.25). Elder brother's person *and* his gold ("I spent whole hours in looking upon it; I told the guineas over and over a thousand times a day." [p.26]) intertwine sexual and social necessity, so that in Moll's rendering sexual and social movement are reciprocally engulfing, one cooperating with the other, each finally indistinguishable from the other.

Moll, of course, rushes by these implications, translating this unifying cooperation of socio-economic and sexual desire into a missed and misunderstood opportunity. But she does understand as she looks back that she and her seducer were both in their own way innocent, each unaware of the other's psychological and social location, unable to read accurately the motives Moll retrospectively sees as given so obviously by a supervising network of socio-economic relationships:

> Nothing was ever so stupid on both Sides, had I acted as became me, and resisted as Vertue and Honour requir'd, this Gentlman had either Desisted his Attacks, finding no room to expect the Accomplishment of his Design, or had made fair, and honourable Proposals of Marriage; in which Case, whoever had blam'd him, no Body could have blam'd me. In short, if he had known me, and how easy the Trifle he aim'd at, was to be had, he would have troubled his Head no farther, but have given me four or five Guineas, and have lain with me the next time he had come at me; and if I had known his Thoughts, and how hard he thought I would be to be gain'd, I might have made my own Terms with him. (pp.25–26)

Moll recounts both her immersion in these complex circumstances and her acquired sense of how to manage a tactical apartness from them. In her formal capacity as narrator, Moll is necessarily forced to balance her character's instinctive tactical awareness against a coherent and inescapable fate that she knows looms constantly. Indeed, by their variety and inventiveness these tactical moves for survival point to a supervising totality, a fate merely postponed. Retrospective narration like hers produces a knowledge of experience by treating it as both freely chosen or at least freely adaptive behavior and fatefully circumscribed and fully determined, so that the pattern of her life constitutes what Marxists call an inclusive contradiction whose poles presuppose each other.

Such contradiction is richly enacted in the climax of the narrative, the Newgate episode. What Moll experiences in Newgate is in her rendering exactly what she has hitherto evaded: the massive, inexorable force of psycho-social determinants. Newgate implicitly resolves the paradox of Moll's free but fated movement, forcing her to exchange her free-wheeling movement for a knowledge and experience of what she herself calls inevitable: "It seemed to me that I was hurried on by an inevitable and unseen fate to this day of misery . . . that I was come to the last hour of my life and of my wickedness together. These things pour'd themselves in upon my Thoughts, in a confus'd manner, and left me over-whelm'd with Melancholly and Despair" (p.274). Important here is Moll's recourse to intensely figurative language, Defoe's attempt to evoke metaphorically a scene too full for Moll's customarily knowing and controlling discourse. The experience of Newgate is, first, graphically literal: "the hellish Noise, the Roaring, Swearing and Clamour, the Stench and Nastiness, and all the dreadful croud of Afflicting things that I saw there" (p.274). In due course, Newgate's effects on Moll can be explained only in the most metaphorical passage in the entire narrative:

> Like the Waters in the Caveties, and Hollows of Mountains, which petrifies and turns into Stone whatever they are suffer'd to drop upon; so the continual Conversing with such a crew of Hell-Hounds as I was with had the same common Operation upon me, as upon other People, I degenerated into Stone; I turn'd first Stupid and Senseless, then Brutish and thoughtless, and at last raving Mad as any of them were; and in short, I became as naturally pleas'd and easie with the Place, as if indeed I had been born there. (p.278)

At least for the moment, Moll is completely absorbed by her circumstances, the hitherto self-defining distance between herself and her social relationships cancelled by what she can render only as a natural force. If we think back to Moll's sexual initiation by the elder brother at Colchester, there is an inevitability in this equation of the force of a social institution like Newgate and the transforming power of nature. In the earlier scene, socio-economic determinants (summed up in the thrilling guineas) are absorbed by the natural, compulsive inevitability of sex. Invoking the natural as an ultimate explanatory frame of reference is an ideological strategy for neutralizing the threatening, alienated objectivity of social institutions by shifting their origins to a universalized interiority. But Newgate is not merely rendered as an intense interior experience. Moll is, she insists, literally transformed. She becomes just like her brutish fellow prisoners, "a meer *Newgate-Bird*, as Wicked and Outragious as any of them," but she also becomes thereby someone else, "no more the same thing that I had been, than if I had never been otherwise than what I was now" (p.279). Newgate as a concrete instance of social totality effectively replaces Moll, and that obliteration leads in due course to a newly distinct self, defined now by *opposition* rather than marginalized and subversive participation. Such opposition, it follows, points clearly to the sort of social totality, or at least to the effects of such a totality, we find at the center of much later evocations of social experience in fiction.

Paradoxically, Moll becomes pure object here but also at least an even more powerful and coherently self-conscious subject. Up to now, we may say, what Moll's narrative patches together is a fitful necessity, the intermittent difficulties of survival and obstacles to steady prosperity. What Newgate offers, both as locale and as narrative climax, is a pre-existent and self-sufficient system that functions independently and to whose laws she must conform. *Moll Flanders* thus articulates in this sequence a version of classic bourgeois ideology, wherein as J. M. Bernstein puts it freedom is exiled into interiority, and spontaneity and freedom are the defining human powers, but the exercise of those powers constructs or reveals a world in which such powers are denied.[19] In Newgate Moll finds precisely that world. But she evades the prison's monumental necessity by slowly turning it into a means of narrative coherence, transforming it from the embodiment of social inevitability for born thieves like her to a locale where to preserve itself her personality acquires a desperate coherence and sharp self-definition in opposition to the now visible determining force of state regulation. In place of the scattered, improvised resistance to social necessity Moll has hitherto practiced, Newgate forces her by its totalizing transformation to muster a countervailing transformation.

If the sequence is read carefully, it appears that Moll begins to recover when she sees her Lancashire husband, now a famous highwayman brought to justice at last. As she secretly observes him enter the prison, her sense of her responsibility for his fate restores her abhorrence of Newgate and something like her old identity. In effect, she passes from obliteration by a social totality to restoration within an appropriated version of that totality, a coherence modelled on the fateful ordering Newgate enforces. That is to say, Moll retrospectively uncovers a moment of liberating retrospection; she discovers in Newgate a method of self-construction when she sees Jemy and suddenly perceives a coherent network of guilt and responsibility in her past. Within the totalizing precincts of Newgate, where scattered self-inventiveness has been forced to give way to external social determination, Moll is moved to discover a new, specifically narrative approach to self-understanding. She acts, we may say, in a narrative mode imposed upon her by the experience of the prison. Newgate extracts from Moll what she has only postponed; its confinement brings the experience of the inescapable connection between social circumstances and personality and points implicitly as the resolution of Moll's career to a larger and indeed comprehensive social inevitability.

Moll's repentance, the "freedom of discourse" the minister leads her to, enables her for the first time in her life to tell her story. "In a word, I gave him an abridgement of this whole history; I gave him the picture of my conduct for fifty years in miniature" (p.288). Having experienced Newgate, indeed having become indistinguishable from it, Moll can now experience a subjectivity conscious of its relationship to the necessity Newgate embodies. She is, as she herself says, restored to thinking: "My temper was touched before, the hardened, wretched boldness of spirit which I had acquired abated, and conscious in the prison, guilt began to flow in upon my mind. In short, I began to think, and to think is one real advance from hell to heaven. All that hellish, hardened state and temper of soul . . . is but a deprivation of thought; he that is restored to his power of thinking is restored to himself" (p.281).

But what possible restoration does Moll have in mind? This is, in effect, a new identity, defined and crystallized within Newgate's complex of determining relationships. Confronted with massive, irresistible necessity, Moll constructs an individuality that is dialectically related to the impersonality she has experienced. In response to Newgate's alienated objectivity and impersonal subordination of individuals to the pattern of judicial retribution, Moll discovers in her past a personal connection with other subjects like Jemy and replaces secular conviction and impersonal punishment with personal guilt and responsibility as she shifts the defining acts of her narrative from the violation of external statutes to private offenses against God and particular men. In the Newgate episode of *Moll Flanders*, Defoe dramatizes as nowhere else in his fiction a sense of a determining social totality and something of a solution to the problem it poses for self-understanding. Moll's new mode of self-apprehension accomplishes what is logically impossible but historically both necessary and inevitable in the history of the novel; it constructs a free subject wholly implicated in a determining objectivity. Next to the inconsistent and improbably resilient Moll who enters the prison, this character has a self-conscious psychological density and coherence that are produced or at least provoked by the experience of social totality. This sequence in *Moll Flanders* thus predicts the direction the novel will take in the nineteenth century. As society is increasingly experienced as mysteriously all-encompassing in its determinations, novelistic representation will seek to imagine a compensating richness of subjectivity.

Notes

1 *Commissioned Spirits: The Shaping of Social Motion in Dickens, Carlyle, Melville, and Hawthorne* (New Brunswick, New Jersey: Rutgers University Press, 1979), pp. 5–6.

2 London: Hutchinson, 1983, p. 19.

3 *The Adventures of Ferdinand Count Fathom*, ed. Damian Grant (London: Oxford University Press, 1971), pp. 2–3.

4 Barrel, p. 206.

5 New York: Oxford University Press, 1976, pp. 243–44.

6 *The Nation-State and Violence (Volume Two of A Contemporary Critique of Historical Materialism)* (Berkeley and Los Angeles: University of California Press, 1985), p. 21.

7 P. 44.

8 In *Imagining the Penitentiary: Fiction and the Architecture of Mind in Eighteenth-Century England* (Chicago: Univ. of Chicago Press, 1987), John Bender develops Giddens' ideas about this emerging modern state and the development of the novel. I owe my understanding of this relationship to Bender's provocative and original work.

9 *After Virtue: A Study in Moral Theory*, second edition (Notre Dame, Indiana: University of Notre Dame Press, 1984), p. 32.

10 *The Origins of Modern English Society* (London: Routledge & Kegan Paul, 1969; Ark paperbacks, 1985), p. 51.

11 *The World of Defoe* (London: Weidenfield & Nicolson, 1976), p. 165.

12 *The Versatile Defoe: An Anthology of Uncollected Writings by Daniel Defoe*, ed. Laura Curtis (Totowa, New Jersey: Rowman and Littlefield, 1979), p. 213.

13 Everyman's Library Edition, introductions by G. D. H. Cole and D. C. Browning, 2 vols. (London: J. M. Dent & Sons, 1962), I, 345, 347.

14 *The Complete English Tradesman: Directing him in the several Parts and Progressions of Trade*, 2 vols. (first published 1725–27; third edition, 1732), I, 308.

15 *The Complete English Tradesman*, II, 182, 185.

16 *The Rise of the Novel* (Berkeley and Los Angeles: University of California Press, 1957), p. 60.

17 *Colonel Jack*, ed. Samuel Holt Monk (London: Oxford University Press, 1965), p. 11. All further references in the text are to this edition.

18 *Moll Flanders*, ed. G. A. Starr (London: Oxford University Press, 1971),
    p. 74. All further references in the text are to this edition. Starr notes that in
    The Great Law of Subordination Consider'd (1724) Defoe makes the point about
    the depletion of males that Moll questions here, but that in *Applebee's Journal*
    for April 10, 1725, he suggests that those numbers are matched by the
    emigration of women to the plantations in America.
19 *The Philosophy of the Novel: Lukacs, Marxism and the Dialectics of Form* (Minne-
    apolis: University of Minnesota Press, 1984), p. xvii.

THE DILEMMAS OF GENDER AS DOUBLE-VOICED NARRATIVE; OR, MARIA EDGEWORTH MOTHERS THE BILDUNGSROMAN[1]

Mitzi Myers

"The proper education of a female, whether
for use or for happiness, is still to seek,
still a problem beyond human solution."
Fanny Burney, *Camilla; or, A Picture of
Youth* (1796)

"Oh teach her, while your lessons last,
To judge the present by the past!
The mind to strengthen and anneal,
While on the stithy glows the steel."
*Rosamond: A Sequel to Early
Lessons* (1821)

"Open-hearted and open-mouthed as I am, I
can keep a secret WONDERFUL well."
A Memoir of Maria Edgeworth[2]

CRITICS can no longer assume that important narratives deal with war or whales and that, as Virginia Woolf critiqued their consensus in 1929, "This is an insignificant book because it deals with the feelings of women in a drawing room." The schoolroom remains another matter. If the adult woman's novel has moved uptown, early juvenile fictions of female development still reside in the low rent district, excluded from the canon and relegated to skimpy chapters in histories of children's literature. Yet the gendered themes and narrative strategies and the cultural and psychosexual uses of women's juvenile literature offer rich materials for reconceptualizing the Georgian woman writer and the nature of her achievement. As a complex *Bildungsroman* which enacts its author's as well as its protagonist's coming of age — mothering writer, heroine, and reader alike — Maria Edgeworth's Rosamond stories (1796–1821) illuminate an important and neglected writer, normally praised for her manly public scope and sociological realism when she is read at all. Their dialogic interplay of child and adult, daughter and mother, constitutes a double-voiced narrative of some subtlety and considerable literary moment. The issues that the stories address and the relational literary modes in which their themes are inscribed epitomize a disregarded tradition of women's writing that is neither culturally marginal nor aesthetically uninviting. As mothered texts, the tales imply a revisionary approach toward defining the specificities of women's writing and the strategies by which women evade the "anxiety of authorship" endemic to their sex. These claims for the significance of the miniature emerge clearly when contextualized by the kind of adult fiction such stories typically rewrite.[3]

At the heart of most late-eighteenth-century women's fiction is, in Fanny Burney's classic and much borrowed subtitle, "the history of a young lady's entrance into the world." Even though Burney herself gave high marks to the "new walk" in juvenile literature pioneered by authors like Anna Laetitia Barbauld, Sarah Trimmer, and Maria Edgeworth, we still tend to identify women writers' entry into significant literary production with their sentimental or Gothic elaborations and variants. Burney's *Evelina* made *the* woman's plot — the passage from orphanage or isolation to sensibility rewarded that translates women's cultural marginalization and limited options into a satisfying romantic mythology, love canceling victimization, and marriage concluding the *Bildungsroman*.[4]

In a provocative exploration of gender and genre, for example, G. A. Starr argues that such fictions of female development are conventional and unproblematic, that for women the gap between the sentimental novel and the *Bildungsroman* that he finds characteristic of male texts does not exist. The eighteenth-century girl need never grow up. No "shedding of puerility" is requisite, for "the virtues demanded of her as a woman remain those prized in her as a child" — cultural equations of femininity with susceptible feelings, passivity, innocence, and vulnerability insure a "fundamental continuity . . . between girl and woman." For Starr, then, the late-eighteenth-century feminine *Bildungsroman* can simultaneously remain a sentimental novel as a young man's entrance into the world cannot. A maturing hero would have to leave behind the childishness, stasis, and intense though rather impotent feeling that characterize sentimental fiction; a heroine need not, for her culture (like Lord Chesterfield) defines women as merely "children of a larger growth." "Only A Boy" can be a sentimental hero, but even a grownup heroine can relate her life in the gush of seventeen-year-old sensibility. Though more discreetly phrased, Starr's equation of female *Bildung* with arrested development differs little from Hazlitt's dismissal of Burney's plots as "too much 'Female Difficulties'; they are difficulties created out of nothing" or from Walter Allen's assessment of her artlessness: "a mouse's view of the world of cats" delivered via a "camera eye" and "microphone ear."[5]

Despite perceptive feminist analyses of canonical male assumptions like these, the classic heterosexual romance plot remains problematic as the formal inscription of female *Bildung*. Even when rewritten by Cinderella as subject, other feminist critics suggest, romance emplotment intrinsically denies female option and power. *Evelina* dances in fetters, for romance and *Bildung*, love and mature self-definition, cannot coexist. Finding a husband, discovering a father, Evelina cannot elude patriarchal possession or masculine desire, but remains an object passed from one male hand to another. What Nancy K. Miller terms the eighteenth-century "heroine's text" insistently eroticizes the textual socialization of the female self. Whether "euphoric," like *Evelina's* social integration, or "dysphoric," like *Clarissa's* exclusion and death, denouements derive from seductions evaded or embraced: "*Bildung* tends to get stuck in the bedroom." Limited to female developmental plots where maturation ceases at the altar or is realized but in the coffin, we can only "stop reading novels." Or totally rescript romance: Rachel Blau DuPlessis suggests that not until modernists began to write "beyond the ending" could women evade the "scripts of heterosexual romance, romantic thralldom, and a telos in marriage" that muffle female character and repress fully feminocentric narrative.[6] *Evelina*, then, has been taken as the paradigmatic eighteenth-century female *Bildungsroman*: its maturational pattern and its art somehow puerile when measured by male norms, and whether viewed from a generous or a less sympathetic feminist perspective, its plot and power structures conditioned by men. *Evelina* and *Camilla*, Burney's prototypical novels of female development, are novels of nondevelopment. Their youthful protagonists, however capable of moral insight and growth, are trapped in narrative structures so realistically reiterating feminine powerlessness that their happy courtship resolutions fail to satisfy. The vibrant child cannot be the mother of a woman; she grows down, not up.

Nor do heroines undergoing their crucial initiation into society get help from strong, supportive mothers. Indeed, it is a critical commonplace that "the women novelists of the period from Fanny Burney to Mrs. Gaskell and George Eliot create very few positive images of motherhood"; mothers in the period are "usually bad and living, or good and dead." But if at first glance *Evelina* seems dominated by omnipresent and omnipotent father-tutors, the novel's conclusion is haunted by the missing mother and by obscure intimations of the mature maternal power from which the heroine's entitlement derives. She can be recognized publicly as daddy's girl because she is so visibly her mother's daughter. Like the fairy tale plot it recreates, the Cinderella romance of *Evelina* fosters adolescent initiation through its quasi-magical maternal subtext. Burney's authorial self-imaging suggests the same displacement. Submerging her authority as moral spokeswoman, she aligns herself with the diffidence of her romantic heroines. Should *Evelina* be censured as a "rather bold attempt," it is, after all, just recapitulating a youthful consciousness: "I have not pretended to show the world what it actually *is*, but what it *appears* to a girl of seventeen: and so far as that, surely any girl who is past seventeen may safely do?" Mature wisdom and worldly satire are more safely attributed to male mentors or to the witty older women who may be enjoyed, but must ultimately be disavowed, for Burney "would a thousand times rather forfeit my character as a writer, than risk ridicule or censure as a female." Burney thus doubly embodies the central late-eighteenth-century "tradition of expressing the heroine's sensibilities."[7]

Penetrating the haze of puerility that Starr finds hanging over sentimental fiction, Margaret Anne Doody sees in late-eighteenth-century women writers' work a struggle toward both a new female protagonist and a new narrative strategy that would eventuate in the double-voiced mode of an Austen or an Eliot, the *style indirect libre* which melds grown-up omniscience with the fallible characters' perspective via indirect quotation: the inadequacy of a faulty heroine's view of self and world ruthlessly yet sympathetically judged, the inner life preserved yet objectively situated. Though Doody is little interested in girls' fiction, the same maturational efforts toward an educated, enlightened heroine and a knowledgeable narrative presence characterize juvenile authors. Indeed, it can be argued that the attempt to establish in alternating perspective a judicious female voice and the affective truths of feminine experience is revealed most clearly in those works which aspire, like the Rosamond tales, to demonstrate how the child *can* become the mother of the woman. In its choice of authoritative persona, thematic issues, and narrative mode, Edgeworth's Rosamond sequence reads like an answer to the female dilemmas that Burney's achievement poses, albeit (like most answers) one raising further questions. Though written at wide intervals and originally published in separate collections, the interlinked short stories about Rosamond from *The Parent's Assistant* (1796), *Early*

Lessons (1801), *Continuation of Early Lessons* (1814), and *Rosamond: A Sequel* (1821) add up to a coherent reconceptualization of the female developmental plot.[8]

These tales tracing the growth of an autobiographical heroine from early childhood to adolescence constitute a narrative of development as quintessentially feminine as Burney's *Evelina* and *Camilla*—but rewritten as an overtly mothered text, a prenuptial rather than a patriarchal love plot. Exploring this difference helps illuminate the larger issue of sexual "difference" in writing. Edgeworth's recasting of the heroine's entrance into the world and search for her identity motif is not just the juvenilization of a familiar format, though Rosamond is much involved with the problematics of gendered identity in Georgian society. (She has, for example, a loving but condescending brother whose masculinist pretensions Edgeworth delights in gently mocking.) Foregrounding *Evelina's* subtext of a powerful maternal presence, the Rosamond series can be read as an alternative kind of early feminocentric fiction. Edgeworth replaces the usual heterosexual romance script fusing female self-definition with relations between the sexes by a mother-daughter educational narrative thematizing domestic realism and enlightened choice, dramatizing through its rationally mothered heroine's tutorial adventures how young readers can learn to cope with their culture. Episode after heuristic episode demonstrates that girls need not fall prey to culturally conditioned sensibility and romantic fantasy; that they can indeed think, judge, and act for themselves—phrases that form the leitmotiv of the tales; that sensibility is not of itself a virtue to be rewarded, but must be assimilated to sense within a revised configuration of female possibility.

Take, for example, the earliest and most famous of the stories, the one inevitably cited in histories of children's literature. Called "The Purple Jar," it might just as aptly be styled "the history of a *very* young lady's entrance into the world." Or "First Impressions," for the working name of *Pride and Prejudice* would fit as many of Edgeworth's tales as Austen's novels. With a surety, economy, and sly humor that entitle her to be termed the Jane Austen of the nursery, Edgeworth brings a similar rationality and realism to bear on similar conflicts: the need to distinguish between true and false vision, sentimental illusion and the solid facts of ordinary life. For Burney's social panoramas, melodramatic actions, and beautiful heroines fulfilling exciting fates, Edgeworth's narrower compass, smaller even than Austen's famous two inches of ivory, follows Rosamond from seven to about thirteen; outings, visits, and friends are in plentiful enough supply, but this is a child's world, its settings and dialogues familial especially in the earliest tales, where the whole of the story is the interchange between mother and daughter. (Rosamond's father, like Richard Lovell Edgeworth, is involved in his children's education, but the mother is the initiatory teacher). Literally a youngster's entrance into the bustling world of London, "The Purple Jar" is a parable of female socialization demonstrating for child and adult audience alike how maternal enlightenment fosters rational girlhood. As Rosamond and her mother journey through the crowded streets, Edgeworth takes a reformer's stance toward Georgian consumerism and fashionable display, exemplifies a progressive, experientially based educational method, and compliments junior misses by imagining them capable of reasoned thought. Paradigmatic of all the tales, "The Purple Jar" offers a coherent blueprint for forming a Georgian girl's mind so she can read her culture aright and counter her period's feminine stereotypes.

Rosamond enters the narrative series (as she will conclude it) exclaiming, while her mother as characteristically questions: "Oh! mother, how happy I should be," said she, as she passed a toy-shop, "if I had all these pretty things?" "What, all! Do you wish for them all, Rosamond?" "Yes, mamma, all." Amid the busy streets and crammed shop windows, the plethora of sights and sounds, of playthings, ribbons, lace, blossoms, baubles, jars, Rosamond's bewildered imagination goes window-shopping — "Look, look! blue, green, red, yellow, and purple! Oh, mamma, what beautiful things! . . . if I had money, I would buy roses, and boxes, and buckles, and purple flower-pots, and every thing" (*Works* 11:147–48). Rosamond's immersion graphically depicts the undiscriminating openness to stimuli and inability to make sense of its culture which any small child must resign to become a maturely functioning human being, but her greedy spontaneity also takes a specifically feminine turn. If Rosamond is (as we shall see) Maria Edgeworth, she is also Everygirl, blessed and cursed with those qualities usually attributed to females in her society: expressivity, imagination, a volatile mental set that hops from one thing to another and never stays to connect consequences. Typically, this story centers on a test, a choice that entails a reading of reality: a radiant purple jar in a chemist's window that fancy converts to a flowerpot versus much needed new shoes. Modern critics universally fault the mother, the story, and the author for not simply telling the child that the jar's beautiful color comes only from the liquid it contains, rather than letting her find out for herself. Had Rosamond been fully informed, they suggest, she would have chosen the new shoes and not have had to go slipshod for a month. Besides, even if she did choose amiss, it was downright mean to deny her the shoes for so long.[9]

Yet to reason thus is to miss the point of Edgeworth's delicate social comedy. Rosamond's progress from confused passivity to rational agency must originate in her own observations and attempts to think. She asks no questions despite her mother's promptings that she cannot be "quite sure that you should like the purple vase *exceedingly*, till you have examined it more attentively . . . I want you to think for yourself . . . when you are to judge for yourself, you should choose what will make you the happiest." But like a stereotypical girl, seduced by beauty, glamour, and fashion, use or no use, Rosamond mistakes surface for reality, never focuses her attention, never corrects her first impressions, even though she must remove stones from her worn-out shoe all the way back to the shop to purchase the jar of her fantasy: "often was she obliged to hop with pain; but still the thoughts of the purple flower-pot prevailed, and she persisted in her choice." And so she must take responsibility for it, even if it means waiting a month for new shoes. Edgeworth's woman-centered pedagogic tale insists that a little girl too "must abide by your own choice" if she is to become a self-aware, self-dependent, and responsible woman (*Works* 11:149–50).

Like the whole sequence tracing Rosamond's maturation, and all are ultimately success stories except this first, "The Purple Jar" rewrites cultural stereotypes of females as passive victims at the mercy of external circumstances and their own undisciplined emotions by granting girls potential self-command and rational agency. In one way or another, each tale acts to remedy culturally determined female deficiency in independent thinking and affirms that girls can achieve control of their wits and hence in some measure of their lives. Burney's double register locates feminine potentiality in a world that insists on feminine powerlessness. Scaling the difficulties of female socialization down to a child's level, Edgeworth's stories of progressive education for girls read like a quasi-Wollstonecraftian critique of contemporary women's education and gender definition. They do not deny the difficulties Burney insists on; rather, they make them manageable by miniaturizing them, by offering a repertoire of coping strategies and, more important, a different sense of female selfhood — the rational capabilities underlined by the *Sequel's* epigraph and the tales' insistence that the irrepressibly imaginative and impulsive Rosamond acquire "a taste for truth and realities" (*Works* 11:215). Conjoining a vividly imagined domestic realism rich in details of everyday life with the theme of domestic heroism for girls, the stories show how small choices and "seeming trifles" engender "greater virtues." Suave as Wollstonecraft's polemic is not, Edgeworth's tales nonetheless discreetly echo the *Rights of Woman's* demand that women achieve "power . . . over themselves": girls who acquire "self-command"

and "power over their own minds" may "be left securely to their own guidance."[10]

More can be claimed for Edgeworth's fictional imagination than this appealing surface reading, however. Less limited than the private expressiveness of Evelina's letters, Edgeworth's double-voiced narrative juxtaposes the child's subjective point of view with the mother's instructive commentary and frames both within an enabling myth of the female author as maternal educator. Yet the interplay among the mother who teaches, the infinitely educable daughter whose apprenticeship to reason is denied closure, and the writer who mothers the story generates its own subtext. The abuse that chroniclers of children's literature heap on Rosamond's powerful, "logically minded mother" attests to the problematics of pedagogy: "you hate the mother. . . . You know she is right, and you loathe rectitude accordingly." Rosamond "is irresistible. It is her Mother who represents Theory"; Rosamond "is an engagingly real child, impetuous, eager, and generous, well-meaning, and quick to repent. But . . . Rosamond's mother chills. She is in fact the prototype of many rational mothers" in early-nineteenth-century juvenile fiction. "Of course she always wins." "Breathes there a child with soul so dead, that would not to itself have said — 'I hate, I simply *detest* that mother of Rosamond!' That this was not the impression intended to be conveyed is, however, perfectly certain"; the story was meant to celebrate the "triumph of the Perfect Parent; but every child knows it is Rosamond who triumphs." Resistant to eighteenth-century moral purposiveness and residually fearful of maternal power, these modern readers ignore the author's gendered identity as the product of her historical period and her specific relational matrix. Nor do they notice Edgeworth's own textual ambivalances ironizing the manifest rationality of the maternal discourse she sponsors. More attentive to nuance, a recent reviewer who testifies to the tale's continuing appeal for girl readers terms it "wonderfully written and marvellously ambiguous."[11]

Elucidating this ambiguity requires a closer look at the story's double voices, for a complex mother-daughter dynamics is central to its meaning. When mother tongue meets daughter tongue — and Edgeworth's characters always spring to life through their dialogue, two ways of construing the world intersect: foresighted adult and spontaneous child; cognitive and affective styles of knowing; factual observation and felt experience. The mother's very articulation, clipped and attentive to consequences, demonstrates that if life is a series of tests, it is also amenable to control. Severely referential and given to checking free-flowing juvenile chatter with a "What do you mean by . . .," the maternal language appropriates the rationalities of the dominant male discourse to insure the Marianne-like child an education in a new style of heroin-ism: "Don't consult my eyes, Rosamond," and her mother turned away her head. "Use your own understanding, because you will not always have my eyes to see with"; "Moderate your transports, my dear Rosa-mond." The daughter's talk, richly responsive to experience — "I am sorry I can't have every thing I wish," "I don't *know*, mamma, but I *fancy*" — reaches as eagerly for approval and connection: ". . . that is, if you won't think me very silly, mamma"; "Rosamond was very sorry that her mother wanted nothing" (*Works* 11:176, 198, 178, 149, 148). Like Austen's sisters, Edgeworth's fictional pairing of mother-daughter in terms of sense-sensibility explores female self-definition through Geor-gian cultural preoccupations. But the Rosamond tales' implied narrative — of maternal sovereignty and seduction, of an initial daugh-terly submission and a finally achieved relational individualism — connects importantly with key issues in modern feminist thought as well, particularly the work of psychoanalytical revisionists who argue for the primacy and the ambivalence of the mother-daughter bond in woman's emotional life and her developmental journey from symbiotic mirroring toward differentiation.

Widely influential, the work of Nancy Chodorow and Carol Gilligan epitomizes a school of thinking about women which rewrites traditional oedipal narratives of female development to relocate power and conflict from the father to the preoedipal mother, the figure with whom all infants feel themselves symbiotically connected. Attempting to explain "the reproduction of mothering," Chodorow argues that girls do not undergo differentiation from the mother in the same way that boys do, nor does the father achieve full parity with her as girls mature. Rather, even adult women retain more flexible and fluid ego boundaries than do men, experience a lifelong sense of identification and connection with the female parent, and tend to construe reality itself in relational terms: "The basic feminine sense of self is connected to the world, the basic masculine sense of self is separate." Extending Chodorow's schema to moral development theory, Gilligan finds that the sense of empathy built into the primary definition of female selfhood accounts for different ethical as well as psychic narratives, an "overriding concern with rela-tionships and responsibilities" rather than rights. "Women's sense of self," Jean Baker Miller similarly concludes, "becomes very much organized around being able to make and then to maintain affiliations and rela-tionships." Such studies have obvious implications for assessing fictions of female development. Generic definitions of the *Bildungsroman* embody male maturational norms and linear plots directed toward separation and autonomy, though women's more interdependent sense of self has historically been organized around the weaving and maintenance of intimate relationships, especially those of childhood; female individualism tends toward the connected and the contextual.[12]

Paradoxically, then, infantilizing her story of feminine *Bildung* affords Edgeworth perhaps more freedom than Burney enjoyed to explore central female issues of power and dependency, individuation and relatedness, of the need to be loved and the need to act as a moral agent: what might be summed up as the "conflict between nurturance and autonomy" that so many recent feminist theorists have found central not only to mother-daughter dynamics, but also to women's whole sense of themselves. Despite its seeming narrative clarity and obvious moral lesson about growing up rational, the Rosamond series' biographical context and emotional subtext generate dualities of voice and message at once more ambiguous and less pessimistic about the possibilities of mature female self-definition than Burney's beleaguered self in a man's world. The Georgian rational mother is a cultural symbol of female agency and autonomy, but also alterity and psychic distance. Overwriting the daughter's relational needs and expressive "feminine" voice with the sterner language that offers access to culture and power, she is both a figure to emulate and a figure to fear — a historically necessary if not altogether satisfying double for the original mother incorporated within, the unconditionally responsive nurturer whose affection does not have to be earned by achievement. Edgeworth's autobiographical heroine may be the author's daughter and the narrative environment a way to mother herself more satisfyingly than real life has, but the dialogic voices of mother and daughter which, as we shall see, recuperate one family situation carry beyond personal self-definition to illuminate larger questions about gender definition and its literary representation as well. Maria Edgeworth's discourse of the daughter who writes qua mother (and via maternal mediation qua father too) engages lively contemporary issues of women's linguistic practice as well as psychic structure.[13]

Thinking of Edgeworth as a woman writer whose narrative structures textualize the nurturing energies of the mother, developing her own selfhood while educating others, is not simply to feminize the reigning explanatory paradigm of paternal influence — for even more than Fanny Burney, Maria Edgeworth signs herself daddy's girl, soliciting what Richard Lovell calls the "paternal *imprimatur*," his encouragement, his criticism, his prefaces, above all, his love. Rather, it is to situate her work within a more complex family dynamics and to argue for the familial situation as at once instigator and central theme in her educational prose and her fiction, whether for child or adult. All her life, whatever she produced — letter, tract, and tale alike, Edgeworth used the very act of writing itself to weave and maintain familial relationships, which (characteristic of her period and especially of her family) she likes to imagine in pedagogic terms. Pledges of love, her tales were "pen-and-ink children" circulated among a widening family network seeking connection and instruction: she "should be *extremely* obliged to the whole Committee of Education and Criticism at Edgeworthstown, if they would send corrections to me from their own brains" goes a typical comment. Someone is always learning (or failing to learn) something in these stories, "the slight figure of a young person" which opens her last (and best) adult novel, *Helen* (1834), threads through all her work, and her themes invariably foreground the impact of childhood instruction on characters' later lives.[14]

Yet the rather atypical *Castle Rackrent* (1800) — itself an ironized family situation — has towered over any other achievement, just like Maria's flamboyant, much-married father. Whether viewed as enfeebling or enlarging (as her definitive biographer Marilyn Butler and some of Butler's nineteenth-century predecessors have argued), paternal influence has usurped even more space in studies of her work than in her life — no easy feat. Clearly, as she repeatedly testifies, he was a potent inspiriting force. She needed a relational motive to write, whether her father or another of her family: "Without . . . affection I should no more work than a steam engine without fire. . . . *If you take away my motive I cannot move.*" But he was not a literary dictator who forced Maria willynilly to embrace the didactic image typically associated with her work. He was the sole determinant of neither her literary nor her private identity, but a commanding presence within a larger relational field that changed over time, as did his daughter's personality. Appropriately, one late Victorian critic located her as a transitional figure between eighteenth- and nineteenth-century fiction who newly stresses the "gradual development of character in and through action." Just as Edgeworth's adult works partake of the moral tale and structure their themes through family relationships, the best of her children's tales assume this *Bildungsroman* format, informed, like her shrewd and lively letters, with all the "attraction of unconscious autobiography."[15] Paternal and maternal elements, didacticism and self-discovery fuse in her work and in her own evolving life.

To understand Edgeworth's Rosamond tales as a mothered text, a miniaturized psychic autobiography that is at once didactic and autodidactic, we need to review the relational matrix conditioning their authorial stance and narrative shape. Recognizing that minds can think back through fathers or mothers, Virginia Woolf nevertheless maintains that women writers especially "think back through our mothers." Certainly, if

Edgeworth anticipates Scott and the nineteenth-century regional novel — the large-scale sociological recreation of a culture — in many of her tales for mature audiences, she also inherits and mothers a rich female tradition more given to what Gaston Bachelard terms the "miniaturizing imagination." She began her writing career with translating Madame de Genlis on education and inventing children's stories for her father's ever increasing household (twenty-two children by four wives), and her last publication in extreme old age was another juvenile moral tale.[16] Though Louisa May Alcott (also a product of parental educational innovators) is often credited with founding the Arcadian family novel, Edgeworth and her sister teachers earlier evolved the genre. The relationally ordered domestic space and the educative purpose centering such stories afford the female author both private gratification and public permission to write.

Late-eighteenth-century women writers legitimated their vocation by what Richard Lovell Edgeworth succinctly terms "that moral tendency, that alone can justify a female for appearing as an author," but the pleasures of "becoming a heroine" — of winning the handsome prince like Evelina or Elizabeth Bennet — have been better explored than those subtler compensations that inhere in imagining oneself as simultaneously child and adult. Children's fiction, a recent critic provocatively suggests, "has the remarkable characteristic of being about something which it hardly ever talks of": "the impossible relation between child and adult." No less than *Peter Pan*, naturalistic moral tales like the Rosamond series play a double game, the author as enlightened mother-teacher improbably coexistent with the author's fallible child self. Personally rewarding, they sustain fantasies of caring and being cared for as they rework and rewrite the story of the unhappily mothered child within, now more satisfyingly nurtured by the narrative environment that the grown-up author shapes. They also enlist mothering fantasies inherent in pedagogy for more public purposes, enabling their authors to speak with cultural authority. It is not hard to see why the poet Samuel Rogers joked about his period's literary women: "How strange it is that while we men are modestly content to amuse by our writings, women must be didactic. . . . Miss Edgeworth is a schoolmistress in her tales."[17]

If the choice is limiting in some ways, the maternal educator's voice, less diffident than Burney's, is empowering in others. Edgeworth enjoys describing her books as "*minnikin* attempts," "wee-wee stories," the literal equivalent of the diminutive self whom she always depicts in family correspondence, even in old age, as the perennial child Rosamond: "I beg, dear Sophy," she writes her cousin, "you will not call my little stories by the sublime title of 'my works,' I shall else be ashamed when the little mouse comes forth." But this self defined in terms of juvenile imagination and sensibility plays within a more potent public image; for some years Edgeworth maintained an extraordinary reputation as the voice of "practical good sense," an enlightened cultural benefactor having, as Francis Jeffrey put it in the *Edinburgh Review*, "done more good than any other writer male or female of her generation." Her tales ambitiously aimed to instruct not just children and adolescents, but the whole of adult popular and polite culture as well: "to promote . . . the progress of education, from the cradle to the grave."[18]

The rather bleak record of Maria Edgeworth's earliest years and the teenage letters that explore her coming to writing elucidate why she chose the didactic educator's voice and how her choice expresses and helps her manage a personal dilemma that replicates this period's gender dilemmas and aesthetic dilemmas as well, conflicts that might be subsumed under the familiar rubric of sense versus sensibility (or named more newly, rational discourse versus relational need). Born in England in 1768, Edgeworth spent her first fourteen years there except for a two-year sojourn in Ireland during her father's second marriage, to Honora Sneyd; she remembered nothing of Ireland, but a great deal about the attractive, accomplished, and rather icily perfect Honora, who is the prototype for Rosamond's mother in the tales. Self-controlled, rational, interested in scientific and literary matters, Honora managed to inspire boundless devotion and yet epitomize sense. Anna Seward (who never wearied of celebrating her in verse) and several men fell deeply in love with her, including Richard Lovell while he was still unhappily married to Maria's mother, the first and least loved of his wives.[19] Realizing his danger, he fled to France and only returned when he learned of his wife's death in March 1773; he and Honora were married in July, and Maria found herself with a new mother who reserved her warmth of affection for a much loved husband. The *Memoir* records that Maria's "father and Mrs. Honora Edgeworth were, even in her earliest years, perceived to be far, far above every one else," that the child "felt great awe of her at the time. . . . at her first acquaintance with her: she remembered standing by her dressing table and looking up at her with a sudden feeling of 'How beautiful!' " A mix of maternal laxity and paternal disregard, Maria's first years had been very different from the attentive domestic education and the almost obsessive child nurture that would characterize the environment of the later Edgeworth youngsters and her own juvenile protagonists. In contrast to Maria's own indulgent and decidedly unintellectual mother, Honora embodied a progressive maternal ideal. She did not pamper, set high standards, and was invincibly just; Maria initially sought attention with destructive acts, the rebellions of a shy child, but she was soon painfully eager to please, to play "your dutiful Daughter" as her first extant letter is signed.[20]

Honora personified everything that Maria was not, everything that the cool ideal of female perfection threading through so much of her stepdaughter's fiction is and that Maria clearly internalized, making high-minded self-command her official public persona, however oddly at variance with her voluble, volatile plain little self. Energetic, "remarkable for strong powers of reasoning," much interested in education, Honora began the records of authentic childhood experience that figure so largely as both method and ideology in Maria and Richard Lovell's treatise on *Practical Education* (1798), and it was she who originated the first tiny book in the long family series of educational texts, although her husband usually receives the credit. Indeed, Honora is the foremother of the whole educational project finished only in 1825 when Maria published the last of the *Early Lessons* begun almost half a century before. Far more significant than its size suggests, this initial tale served as manifesto and pilot work for the family educational achievement that Maria always valued more highly than her own fictions composed outside the enterprise. Building on the pioneering work of Mrs. Barbauld, the narrative of Honora's *Practical Education: or, The History of Harry and Lucy* (1780) adroitly links a fresh educational psychology to a fresh domestic realism through "pictures of real life" and real children that juvenile readers are invited to identify with (iv). Almost twenty years later, the expository *Practical Education* credited Honora with the central principle of the family program: "that the art of education should be considered as an experimental science," *Practical* merely signifying "brought to the test of experience," not programmatic Benthamite utilitarianism, as commentators who read only the title seem to suppose. And, affectively as well as intellectually exemplary, Honora was very deeply beloved by the father who must surely—Joanna Baillie joked to Scott decades later—have fed his daughter "love powders," so passionate was Maria's partiality for that "first object and motive of my mind," the initially inattentive parent whom her writing eventually transformed to "critic, partner, father, friend" united.[21]

Honora's health was poor; Maria was sent away to boarding school at seven. Her stiff, anxious letters and the restrained, even-handed replies occasion thought, as does the long letter to his eldest daughter that the grieving Richard Lovell wrote from beside his wife's corpse in 1780. Already, he had advised his "Plain enough" child that "real good sense," "a benevolent heart, complying Temper, & obliging manners" were requisite: "by your mother's assistance you might become a very excellent, & an highly improved woman." Now, excusing "your excellent mother" for perhaps too scrupulous a justice toward her stepdaughter, the death-bed message simultaneously insists that the girl be grateful for this "timely restraint" which "yielded fondness towards you only by the exact measure of your conduct," that she enshrine Honora and "fix her excellent image in your mind." The child's extraordinary sensibility and her "inordinate desire to be beloved" are the core — defined for much of her life as the defect — of her character, but with these Rosamond qualities, she also has Rosamond's "ardent, active desire to improve," which, so the stories wishfully say, "made her the darling of her own family."[22] Since Maria wants to become "amiable, prudent, and of USE," what better way than to emulate "the most exalted character of your incomparable mother" so that the daughter too can earn the praise which Honora's steady rectitude "forces from the virtuous and the wise." No wonder the *Memoir* records that the letter made the intended impression, that Maria "recollected all her life the minutest advice which Mrs. Honora Edgeworth gave to her," or that the wish to enact her father's counsel "became the exciting and controlling power over the whole of her future life." R. L. Edgeworth would marry happily twice more, and though a year younger than Maria, Frances Beaufort, his last wife, became her best friend and "Dearest Mother" for over forty years, delightfully given to the petting Honora withheld; but to the father Honora seems always to have remained the one woman who "equalled the picture of perfection, which existed in my imagination."[23]

Advised by Honora before her death to marry her younger sister (oblique testimony to the woman's strength of mind), Richard Lovell did so before 1780 was over. By mid-1782, Maria's boarding school exile from home, always one of the most resonant words in her vocabulary, was over, and the whole family permanently settled in Ireland. In the early eighties, Maria probably received proportionately more of her father's attention than she ever got again as Richard Lovell supplemented her formal education, trained her in the business of the estate, and set her writing tasks. Busy with childbirth and child care, Elizabeth Sneyd was not the intellectual companion that her sister had been, and the full scale educational project with an eye to publication lapsed until Maria's work revived it in the nineties. This period's unpublished correspondence to Fanny Robinson, Maria's school friend who "defended me" "where no one liked me," captures the psychic dynamics underlying Maria's self-invention as an educational author and suggests the rich uses of children's literature for the woman writer. Indeed, it can be argued that Edgeworth's letter-writing (she wrote over 2,000 to her family alone) initiates, frames, and ultimately completes the personal *Bildungsroman* that she never permits full closure in the Rosamond tales themselves. Only after her father's death — and perhaps most richly in the vibrant letters where she lets her life round out her art — does she fully integrate the voices of impulsive daughter and knowing mother, sensibility and sense, whose dialogue is the basic structural unit of her fictional autobiography. (It is noteworthy that Edgeworth's most considered appraisal typically images her novelistic art as dialogue, talk, and that the letter and the moral tale similarly encode in their form a relational motive and a dyadic interaction.) Edgeworth's late letters evoke the matriarch, the head of the clan, who is simultaneously her stepmother's beloved daughter, the "old petted nursling" of her "Dearest Mother," and the passionately loving surrogate mother of that stepmother's eldest daughter, the symbolically named Frances Maria; these epistolary texts wholeheartedly enact the loving maternal discourse that eluded the unempathetically mothered child Maria and that the grown-up author's autobiographic mother-daughter fictions more equivocally realize[24] (*Memoir* 3:194).

If Edgeworth's maturest letters heal the linguistic and emotional disjunction between child and adult that her narrative renderings contingently bridge, her early letters adumbrate the dyadic voices whose interaction weaves the story of her juvenile *Bildungsroman*: the exuberant child Rosamond, hungry for love and anxiously improving herself to earn it, and the all wise, antisentimental mother, appropriating (like Honora) the rational language of the dominant male discourse, the former characterized by her ready emotional and imaginative responsiveness, the latter by her carefully considered process of judgment. Through the letters' stilted seriousness or forced sprightliness (both distinct from Edgeworth's mature epistolary voice), the girl struggles to define herself — "Proteus-like I assume different shapes" — and to discover a vocation that will satisfy her needs for relation and achievement. She has a powerful homegrown model of selfhood, for what better way to consolidate her position with her father than to incorporate the missing mother, to become in some sense Honora?

But the letters also consider more public — and in some sense opposed — models of female authorship: Madame de Genlis, the prototypical rational mother-educator, whose *Adèle et Théodore; ou, Lettres sur L'Éducation* she is excitedly translating ("I am writing a book. — A BOOK!"), and Fanny Burney, whose Lord Orville delights her and whose acquaintance and correspondence the teenager daydreams of acquiring, even though she fears novels act on the mind "as Drams do . . . on the body." Letter after letter, Burney "still runs in my head," but these letters also underscore the dilemma of the plain, small girl painfully aware that she lacks Evelina's graces and beauty's power: "with every *personal* disadvantage . . . I know their value, for I know the want of them." *Evelina's* Cinderella closure deceives girl readers, Maria concludes, defining herself not as romantic heroine, but as *philosophe* in phrases that thread through the mother's language in the Rosamond tales: "surely there is nothing ridiculous in a girl of fifteen's attending to the feelings of her own mind and endeavoring to find out what tends to make her more or less happy & what does a philosopher do more." Edgeworth's assumption of the educator's persona conjoins reasoned language and girlish need; to teach is to acquire a father and a mother for oneself. Reviving and completing the family educational project, she connected herself with Richard Lovell, achieved Honora-like status within the family, and found an authoritative public voice. The didactic "plain, practical sense" dispensed by the "Franklin of novelists" was, paradoxically, relationally generated.[25]

Yet though the woman writer can solve the problem of authority by appropriating reason as a mother tongue, the juvenile writer who is a good mother to her character and herself must also find a place for expressivity and the affective truths of female experience within that dominant discourse. Speaking in the rational mother's voice may censor the woman within, but Edgeworth's juvenilia textualize subversive energies as well as moral lessons. Radically opposing critical assessments suggest the complexity of the Rosamond sequence. For P. H. Newby, the heroine is the sole "rebel in this world of common sense," forever resolving to be more foresighted, forever failing to tame her uncalculating love of life; for Marilyn Butler, who tries to draw a sharp contrast between Maria's self-renderings in her last adult novel, *Helen*, and her earlier juvenile representations, Rosamond must be hopelessly inept, a study in "humility, almost self-abasement," recurrently saved from the disastrous consequences of her imprudence by the "watchful despotism of a parent." Neither is correct — nor wholly incorrect, for Edgeworth's complex mothering of her child's text allows her to have her maturation and elude it too. Philippe Ariès and his fellow researchers in family history have been confirming for some years now that adults invented children, that childhood, like gender, is a cultural construct; looking sympathetically and usually very clear-sightedly at actual children, reformist educators like Honora and Richard Lovell fashioned the child to insure progress, reinventing the future adult as well.[26] But if educators invent children, children turned educators invent juvenile selves that simultaneously support and subvert parental premises.

It is every way significant that Maria chose to encode her own personal narrative of female *Bildung* within the family series of educational tales and to make her alter ego a child character, the very epitome of those juvenile and feminine qualities that her culture (and ours) would range against the *philosophe's* reason. Valorizing the literary miniature in the shape of a child's story, her tales about the problems of judgment and conduct that would face any young girl in everyday family life merge the symbolic dimensions of the small: its capacity to act as "metaphor for the interior space and time of the bourgeois subject," to function self-referentially, and its status as a "dominated" world, a model wherein larger-scale problems can be safely manipulated. Once we set aside preconceptions about the juvenile moral tale's transparency as genre, Edgeworth's dual reconceptualizations of the female developmental plot emerge as fantasies of power indulged within domesticated boundaries — the satisfaction of rational achievement, the fulfillment of relational need. Exploiting the powers of the weak, she at once maintains parental love and attention and sustains selfhood. The storyteller's simultaneously aligning herself with sense *and* sensibility realizes a richer model of female selfhood than the tales' direct statement; the implications of her fictional practice round out the standards she endorses. The maternal writer teases and teaches her juvenile self in the interest of more rational girl readers, but writing as a daughter she celebrates that self's imaginative energy and affective needs; better than her mothers real or represented inside the text, the author as mother understands and nurtures the author as daughter.

The story's polemic message valorizes reason and prudent womanhood; that public moral is problematized by its emotional subtext and its exuberant narrative rendering of the errant heroine's perspective, thought processes, and talk, her characteristic volubility and tics of language ("Hey, mamma?") — all the qualities that have won Rosamond renown as the first real living and breathing child in English juvenile literature. Embodying dependence, her need for approval and her very language in its insistent search for connection enacting the relational thinking said to characterize women, Maria's Rosamond nevertheless unmistakably dominates the texts in which she figures. Patterning reality, eliminating the aleatory, the rational narrative logic runs one way, but Rosamond's vivid portrait and ebullient voice tug the reader's attention and heart another direction. Like all the young readers who have seen in her "ever fluctuating mind, an image of their own," we too identify with "her infinite variety of faults, follies, and foibles."[27] The mother earns our respect; Rosamond wins our love.

Writing as at once the daughter of mothers and the mother of daughters, Edgeworth enjoys the opposed gratifications that children's literature paradoxically, perhaps uniquely, permits: wise maturity and positive regression, the fantasies of imaginative self-expression and the rewards of self-restraint. Insistently underlining the mother's power and rationality, the daughter's educability and maturation, the Rosamond series thoughtfully qualifies each as well. It weighs more precisely and more equably than it ever explicitly acknowledges the benefits and the costs of rational womanhood. However much Rosamond learns and improves within the sequence, she also remains irreducibly, unchangeably herself. With its wonderfully realistic final words, a conclusion that denies closure, "The Purple Jar" foreshadows the way the whole series will stop: "Oh, mamma . . . how I wish that I had chosen the shoes . . . however, I am sure—no, not quite sure—but, I hope, I shall be wiser another time." The juvenile tales' prenuptial plot writes finis when Rosamond answers nosy old Lady Worral's anticipated question, *"Ma'am, when will Miss Rosamond's education be finished?"* with "Never while she lives!" (*Works* 11:151, 392).

Ironically, the more literally the heroine fulfills the Edgeworthian parent's injunctions to improve continually, to embrace the real, to restrain sensibility, the more she subverts the premises to which she defers. To represent the real is to represent the true inner juvenile, "feminine" self that is Rosamond; forever to improve is not to become the grown-up rational mother, but eventually to progress beyond her toward a self-definition that unites sense and sensibility, daughter and mother, in a Maria Edgeworth grown up at last—on her own terms, in the domestic life that mattered most to her. Well aware of the gap between her public face and private self, Maria once confessed to Elizabeth Inchbald, "Would you ever have guessed that the character of Rosamond is like ME? All who know me intimately, say that it is as like as it is possible; those who do not know me intimately, would never guess it," and her letters abound in amused references to her own Rosamond qualities, impatience, impulsiveness, enthusiasm, expressiveness, impressionability, a fondness for "being loved," nonsense, laughing, and building castles in the air that lasted past "Rosamond at sixty" into her eighties: "Love me and laugh at me as you have done many is the year."[28] Fittingly, the *Memoir's* final assessment memorializes Maria's personal *Bildungsroman*: "The most remarkable trait in her character was the prudence with which she acted; the command which she had acquired over her naturally impetuous nature and boundless generosity of spirit"; "She had amazing power of control over her feelings when occasion demanded, but in general her tears or her smiles were called forth by every turn of joy and sorrow among those she lived with." Edgeworth's fictional and actual maturational patterns imply that woman's access to rational discourse may be bought with a price, but her achievement also testifies that relational needs must be met too. Well might she assert,

"Reasonable or unreasonable I know my little self."[29] Exploring the latent and manifest content of her juvenile narrative richly expands our sense of women's contribution to the eighteenth-century idea of the novel.

Notes

1 Research for this project has been supported by grants from the National Endowment for the Humanities and the American Philosophical Society.

2 Frances Burney, *Camilla; or, A Picture of Youth* (1796), ed. Edward A. and Lillian D. Bloom (London: Oxford University Press, 1972), p. 357; Maria Edgeworth, *Rosamond: A Sequel to Early Lessons*, 2 vols. (London: R. Hunter; Baldwin, Cradock, and Joy, 1821), epigraph; Maria Edgeworth, *A Memoir of Maria Edgeworth, with a Selection from Her Letters by the Late Mrs. Edgeworth*, ed. by her children, 3 vols. (London: privately printed by Joseph Masters and Son, 1867), 3:187 (10 October 1838).

3 Virginia Woolf, *A Room of One's Own* (1929) (New York and Burlingame: Harcourt, Brace and World, 1957), p. 77. The governing themes of Marilyn Butler's lovingly researched *Maria Edgeworth: A Literary Biography* (Oxford: Clarendon Press, 1972) typify these trends in Edgeworth criticism, as does George Watson's description of Edgeworth as the "least feminine of female novelists," introduction, *Castle Rackrent*, by Maria Edgeworth (1800), World's Classics (Oxford: Oxford University Press, 1980), p. x. Harold Bloom's paradigm of the individual artist's relation to the tradition is revised in Sandra M. Gilbert and Susan Gubar, *The Madwoman in the Attic: The Woman Writer and the Nineteenth-Century Literary Imagination* (New Haven and London: Yale University Press, 1979), p. 49 and *passim*.

4 *Evelina; or, The History of a Young Lady's Entrance into the World* (1778), ed. Edward A. Bloom (London: Oxford University Press, 1970). A typical example of popular juvenile appropriations is [Sarah Green], *Mental Improvement for A Young Lady on Her Entrance into the World: Addressed to A Favorite Niece* (1793), new ed. (London: William Lane, Minerva Press, 1796). Frances Burney D'Arblay, *Diary and Letters of Madame D'Arblay (1778–1840)*, ed. Charlotte Barrett, intro. Austin Dobson, 6 vols. (London: Macmillan, 1904), 5:419.

5 G. A. Starr, " 'Only A Boy': Notes on Sentimental Novels," *Genre* 10 (Winter 1977): 524. *Lord Chesterfield's Letters to His Son and Others*, intro. R. K. Root, Everyman's Library, 1929 (London: Dent; New York: Dutton, 1963), p. 66 (to his son, 5 September 1748). William Hazlitt's comment in *Lectures on the English Comic Writers*, 1819 (Garden City, New York: Doubleday, n. d.), p. 177, refers to the subtitle of Frances Burney D'Arblay's last novel, *The Wanderer; or, Female Difficulties*, 5 vols. (London: Longman, Hurst, Rees,

Orme, and Brown, 1814). Walter Allen, *The English Novel: A Short Critical History* (New York: E. P. Dutton, 1954), p. 96.

6 For an overview of recent Burney criticism, see Roger D. Lund, "The Modern Reader and the 'Truly Feminine Novel,' 1660-1815: A Critical Reading List," *Fetter'd or Free? British Women Novelists, 1670-1815*, ed. Mary Anne Schofield and Cecilia Macheski (Athens and London: Ohio University Press, 1986), pp. 409-12, especially the analyses of Susan Staves, "*Evelina*; or, Female Difficulties," *Modern Philology* 73 (May 1976): 368-81; Judith Lowder Newton, *Women, Power, and Subversion: Social Strategies in British Fiction, 1778-1860* (Athens: University of Georgia Press, 1981), pp. 23-54; and Rose Marie Cutting, "Defiant Women: The Growth of Feminism in Fanny Burney's Novels," *SEL: Studies in English Literature 1500-1900* 17 (Summer 1977): 519-30. Feminist studies too recent to be listed in Lund include Judy Simons, *Fanny Burney*, Women Writers (Totowa, New Jersey: Barnes and Noble, 1987); and Kristina Straub, *Divided Fictions: Fanny Burney and Feminine Strategy* (Lexington: University Press of Kentucky, 1987). Oddly, in the same volume with Lund, Martha G. Brown, "Fanny Burney's Feminism: Gender or Genre?", pp. 29-39, attempts to attribute Burney's characteristic preoccupations solely to her use of romance conventions. Nancy K. Miller, *The Heroine's Text: Readings in the French and English Novel, 1722-1782* (New York: Columbia University Press, 1982), pp. 4, 157-58; Rachel Blau DuPlessis, *Writing Beyond the Ending: Narrative Strategies of Twentieth-Century Women Writers* (Bloomington: Indiana University Press, 1984), p. 2.

7 The missing mother motif is summed up by Susan Peck MacDonald, "Jane Austen and the Tradition of the Absent Mother," *The Lost Tradition: Mothers and Daughters in Literature*, ed. Cathy N. Davidson and E. M. Broner (New York: Frederick Ungar, 1980), p. 58; and Janet Todd, *Women's Friendship in Literature* (New York: Columbia University Press, 1980), p. 2; for perceptive comments on the mother in *Evelina*, see MacDonald's essay, and Mary Poovey, "Fathers and Daughters: The Trauma of Growing Up Female," *Men by Women*, ed. Janet Todd, *Women and Literature*, n.s. 2 (New York and London: Holmes and Meier, 1981), pp. 39-58; Claire Kahane, "The Gothic Mirror," *The (M)other Tongue: Essays in Feminist Psychoanalytic Interpretation*, ed. Shirley Nelson Garner, Claire Kahane, and Madelon Sprengnether (Ithaca and London: Cornell University Press, 1985), pp. 334-51, tracks spectral mothers in eighteenth-century women's Gothic fiction. Frances Burney D'Arblay, *Diary*, 1:22, 162; Jane Spencer, *The Rise of the Woman Novelist: From Aphra Behn to Jane Austen* (Oxford and New York: Basil Blackwell, 1986), p. 96. The feminist and antifeminist literature on Cinderella (and other fairy tales) is very large; for a start on overviews and maternal elements, see Alan Dundes, *Cinderella: A Casebook* (New York: Wildman Press, 1983); and Jack Zipes, ed., *Don't Bet on the Prince: Contemporary Feminist Fairy Tales in North America and England* (New York: Methuen, 1986). The most detailed explications of Burney's achievement are

Simons's, Straub's, and Patricia Meyer Spacks's rather despairing
"Dynamics of Fear: Fanny Burney," *Imagining A Self: Autobiography and Novel
in Eighteenth-Century England* (Cambridge: Harvard University Press, 1976),
pp. 158–92; for a perceptive but similarly bleak reading of *Camilla*, see
Coral Ann Howells, " 'The Proper Education of a Female . . . Is Still to
Seek': Childhood and Girls' Education in Fanny Burney's *Camilla; or, A
Picture of Youth*," *British Journal for Eighteenth-Century Studies* 7 (Autumn 1984):
191–98.

8 The general critical neglect of eighteenth-century women's juvenile writing
results in its omission from such useful recent studies of how women
acquired an authoritative public voice as Margaret Anne Doody, "George
Eliot and the Eighteenth-Century Novel," *Nineteenth-Century Fiction* 35 (Dec.
1980): 260–91; Spencer; and Nancy Armstrong, "The Rise of Feminine
Authority in the Novel," *Novel: A Forum on Fiction* 15 (Winter 1982): 127–45.
Indeed, even when Armstrong's recent book, *Desire and Domestic Fiction: A
Political History of the Novel* (New York and Oxford: Oxford University Press,
1987), briefly mentions the Edgeworths' "highly influential *Practical Educa-
tion*," p. 15, Richard Lovell is cited as Robert and the treatise is misdated
1801 rather than 1798. The first and best known of the Rosamond stories,
"The Purple Jar," was originally part of the 1796 first edition of *The Parent's
Assistant*, but was moved to join new pieces in *Early Lessons*, 10 parts in 6
vols. (London: J. Johnson, 1801). Rosamond gradually grows up in *Continuation of Early Lessons*, 2 vols. (London: J. Johnson, 1814) and *Rosamond: A
Sequel* (1821). An older Rosamond also appears in the adult novel *Patronage*,
4 vols. (London: J. Johnson, 1814). All the Rosamond fictions except
Patronage and "The Birth-Day Present" are published together in *Works of
Maria Edgeworth*, 13 vols. (Boston: Samuel H. Parker, 1825), 11:146–392;
subsequent references incorporated into the text refer to this edition. For the
missing story, see *The Parent's Assistant*, 3rd ed. of 1800 ed., 6 vols. in 2,
Classics of Children's Literature, 1621–1932 (New York: Garland, 1976),
vol. 2 in vol. 1:1–45.

9 The feminine enthusiasm for London's finery, including illuminated displays of "crystal flasks," in visitor Sophie V. La Roche's journal, *Sophie in
London, 1786: Being the Diary of Sophie V. La Roche*, trans. Clare Williams,
1933, Life and Letters Series 72 (London and Toronto: Jonathan Cape,
1936), pp. 86–87, 140–43, accords neatly with Edgeworth's portrayal, as do
the essays in Neil McKendrick, John Brewer, and J. H. Plumb, *The Birth of
a Consumer Society: The Commercialization of Eighteenth-Century England*
(Bloomington: Indiana University Press, 1982). Edgeworth owed much of
her high contemporary reputation to her six volumes of satiric *Tales of
Fashionable Life* (London: J. Johnson, 1809; 1812). Critiquing Edgeworth's
rational tale in her staunchly Anglican *Guardian of Education*, Sarah Trimmer
underscores Edgeworth's point about Rosamond's autonomy even as she
seeks to subvert it. More clearsighted than many modern objectors, she
recognizes that the story affirms the central tenet of the Edgeworths' educa-

tional treatise, *Practical Education* (1798)—"that children should be left to their own sensations and experience . . . instead of being guided in their choice by the opinion of others"—and that the mother's direct guidance would negate the daughter's struggle toward enlightened choice. Had Rosamond been taught the "precepts of Christianity," Trimmer suggests, she would have "acquired beforehand the habit of seeking the advice of her parents, and of submitting to it as a guide for her inexperience. . . . yielding to her mother's advice," *The Guardian of Education; Consisting of a Practical Essay on Christian Education . . . and a Copious Examination of Modern Systems of Education, Children's Books, and Books for Young Persons*, 5 vols. (London: J. Hatchard, 1802-6), 2:235-36. Trimmer's lengthy analyses of all Edgeworth's educational works in the *Guardian*, the first journal devoted to reviewing writing for the young, testify to Edgeworth's popularity and literary merit as well as to the threat her secular ethic was felt to pose.

10 These aspects of the Rosamond stories are situated in their cultural and literary background in my " 'A Taste for Truth and Realities': Early Advice to Mothers on Books for Girls," *Children's Literature Association Quarterly* 12 (Fall 1987): 118-24; the quotation in the title comes from another of the Rosamond stories. Edgeworth's preface to *Rosamond: A Sequel*, 1:vi-vii, parallels Mary Wollstonecraft, *A Vindication of the Rights of Woman, with Strictures on Political and Moral Subjects*, 1792, ed. Charles W. Hagelman, Jr., The Norton Library (New York: W. W. Norton, 1967), p. 107. Though he is not interested in her juvenile writing, Iain Topliss, "Mary Wollstonecraft and Maria Edgeworth's Modern Ladies," *Études Irlandaises* 6 (1981): 13-31, sketches some of the parallels between Wollstonecraft's and Edgeworth's thinking about women, a start toward a more comprehensive analysis of Edgeworthian feminism.

11 F. J. Harvey Darton, *Children's Books in England: Five Centuries of Social Life*, 1932, 3rd. ed., rev. by Brian Alderson (Cambridge: Cambridge University Press, 1982), p. 141; F[lorence] V. Barry, *Maria Edgeworth: Chosen Letters* (Boston and New York: Houghton Mifflin, [1931]), p. 11; Gillian Avery, with the assistance of Angela Bull, *Nineteenth-Century Children: Heroes and Heroines in English Children's Stories 1780-1900* (London: Hodder and Stoughton, 1965), pp. 25-26; Emily Lawless, *Maria Edgeworth*, English Men of Letters Series (London: Macmillan, 1904), p. 56; F[lorence] V. Barry, *A Century of Children's Books*, 1922 (New York: George H. Doran, [1924]), p. 185. Further examples of hostile attitudes toward Rosamond's mother include Alfred Ainger, "The Children's Books of a Hundred Years Ago," *Lectures and Essays*, 2 vols. (London: Macmillan, 1905), 1:382-407; Eveline C. Godley, "A Century of Children's Books," *Living Age*, 7th series, 31 (16 June 1906): 689-98; Marion Lochhead, "Social History in Miniature: Domestic Tales for Children," *Quarterly Review* 291 (Oct. 1953): 516-30; and Elfrida Vipont, "Old Stories Never Die," *Junior Bookshelf* 22 (Nov. 1958): 245-55. Alan Tucker's daughter enjoyed the story very recently, "History and Harvey Darton," *Signal* 38 (May 1982): 113-28; numerous examples of

enthusiastic child readers a century and half ago are scattered through the letters edited by Edgar MacDonald, *The Education of the Heart: The Correspondence of Rachel Mordecai Lazarus and Maria Edgeworth* (Chapel Hill: University of North Carolina Press, 1977), and Samuel Henry Romilly, *Romilly-Edgeworth Letters 1813–1818* (London: John Murray, 1936). A mother in the latter writes, for example: "*Rosamond* has always been a most distinguished favorite. Perhaps they feel a sympathy with her faults and feel that they resemble her," p. 83.

12 Nancy Chodorow, *The Reproduction of Mothering: Psychoanalysis and the Sociology of Gender* (Berkeley: University of California Press, 1978), p. 169; Carol Gilligan, *In A Different Voice: Psychological Theory and Women's Development* (Cambridge: Harvard University Press, 1982), pp. 16–17; Jean Baker Miller, *Toward a New Psychology of Women* (Boston: Beacon, 1976), p. 61. If the *Bildungsroman* itself remains a protean genre despite the many attempts to define it (the 1986 MLA convention devoted a session to yet another attempt to do so), its female variants are still more problematic. For a useful overview of women's developmental fictions in relation to both male definitions and revisionist theory, see the introduction to Elizabeth Abel, Marianne Hirsch, and Elizabeth Langland, eds., *The Voyage In: Fictions of Female Development* (Hanover and London: University Press of New England, 1983).

13 My argument here can only briefly summarize part of a longer study. Although my analysis draws upon revisionist theory — such as that of Jane Flax, "The Conflict Between Nurturance and Autonomy in Mother-Daughter Relationships and Within Feminism," *Feminist Studies* 4 (June 1978): 171–89; Chodorow's work, including "Family Structure and Feminine Personality," *Women, Culture, and Society*, ed. Michelle Zimbalist Rosaldo and Louise Lamphere (Stanford University Press, 1974), pp. 43–65; "Feminism and Difference: Gender, Relation, and Difference in Psychoanalytic Perspective," *Socialist Review* 9 (July-Aug. 1979): 51–69; "Toward a Relational Individualism: The Mediation of Self Through Psychoanalysis," *Reconstructing Individualism: Autonomy, Individuality, and the Self in Western Thought*, ed. Thomas C. Heller, Morton Sosna, and David E. Wellbery (with Arnold I. Davidson, Ann Swidler, and Ian Watt) (Stanford: Stanford University Press, 1986), pp. 197–207; and Gilligan's, including "The Conquistador and the Dark Continent: Reflections on the Psychology of Love," *Daedalus* 113 (Summer 1984): 75–95; "Remapping the Moral Domain: New Images of the Self in Relationship," in *Reconstructing Individualism*, pp. 237–52; "Moral Orientation and Moral Development," *Women and Moral Theory*, ed. Eva Feder Kittay and Diana T. Meyers (Totowa, New Jersey: Rowman and Littlefield, 1987), pp. 19–33 — it is also an attempt to counter criticisms of their work for its ahistoricism and its inattention to the literary dimension of female experience, and to do so without embracing theories of language which allocate the linguistic realm to men and deprive women of discursive possibility. Thoughtful critiques of Chodorow's and

Gilligan's positions include Judith Lorber, Rose Laub Coser, Alice S. Rossi, and Nancy Chodorow, "On *The Reproduction of Mothering:* A Methodological Debate," *Signs: Journal of Women in Culture and Society* 6 (Spring 1981): 482–514; Nina Baym, "The Madwoman and Her Languages: Why I Don't Do Feminist Literary Theory," *Tulsa Studies in Women's Literature* 3 (Spring-Fall 1984): 45–59; Debra Nails, Mary Ann O'Loughlin, and James C. Walker, eds., *Social Research* 50 (Autumn 1983): special issue on "Women and Morality"; Judith Kegan Gardiner, "Maternal Metaphors, Women Readers, and Female Identity, or Mothering Theory, Self Psychology, and Women's Literary Relationships," unpublished essay, Modern Language Association Convention, 1985 (cited by permission); and Linda K. Kerber, Catherine G. Greeno, Eleanor E. Maccoby, Zella Luria, Carol B. Stack, and Carol Gilligan, "Viewpoint: On *In A Different Voice*: An Interdisciplinary Forum," *Signs* 11 (Winter 1986): 304–33. Useful overviews of the burgeoning literature on mothering include Marianne Hirsch, "Mothers and Daughters," *Signs* 7 (Autumn 1981): 200–22; Judith Kegan Gardiner, "Mind Mother: Psychoanalysis and Feminism," *Making a Difference: Feminist Literary Criticism*, ed. Gayle Greene and Coppélia Kahn (New York and London: Methuen, 1985), pp. 113–45; the essays in Garner et al., *The (M)other Tongue*; Domna C. Stanton, "Difference on Trial: A Critique of the Maternal Metaphor in Cixous, Irigaray, and Kristeva," *The Poetics of Gender*, ed. Nancy K. Miller (New York: Columbia University Press, 1986), pp. 157–82; and Beth Kowaleski-Wallace, "Milton's Daughters: The Education of Eighteenth-Century Women Writers," *Feminist Studies* 12 (Summer 1986): 275–93. Most feminist critics would surely agree that "it is time to learn, to begin to speak our mother tongue" (Garner et al., *The (M)other Tongue*, p. 29), but since maternal discourse is a historical product, that tongue may vary by period. Georgian women writers' valorization of the rational makes their maternal figures (like Austen's heroines) anything but preoedipally inarticulate, nor are they sentimental like nineteenth-century mothers. Neither can it be argued (as does Kowaleski-Wallace) that Georgian rational women are simply "Milton's Daughters" who have embraced patriarchal paradigms and write in the father tongue; for a recent revisionist study of Milton and eighteenth-century women which offers a more enabling paradigm, see Joseph Wittreich, *Feminist Milton* (Ithaca and London: Cornell University Press, 1987). Rather, I would argue that if, as Eagleton, Todd, and Richardson demonstrate, Georgian male writers colonized the conventionally feminine domain of sensibility for their own purposes, women writers similarly appropriated conventionally masculine rationality to support their own educational and cultural claims; see Terry Eagleton, *The Rape of Clarissa: Writing, Sexuality, and Class Struggle in Samuel Richardson* (Minneapolis: University of Minnesota Press, 1982); Janet Todd, *Sensibility: An Introduction* (London and New York: Methuen, 1986); and Alan Richardson, "Romanticism and the Colonization of the Feminine," *Romanticism and Feminism*, ed. Anne K. Mellor (Bloomington: Indiana University Press, 1988).

Since, as Joan W. Scott observes, gender is a primary way of signifying relationships of power, educators who interpret gender as a cultural construct rather than an essentialist given inevitably make use of their period's discourse of power ("Gender: A Useful Category of Historical Analysis," *American Historical Review* 91 [Dec. 1986]: 1069). The mother tongue of Georgian women educators strives to combine rationality and objectivity with nurturance and caring, to unite what Mary Field Belenky, Blythe McVicker Clinchy, Nancy Rule Goldberger, and Jill Mattuck Tarule, *Women's Ways of Knowing: The Development of Self, Voice, and Mind* (New York: Basic Books, 1986), would term procedural and subjective knowledge or what Gilligan describes as "a language of love that encompasses both knowledge and feelings" ("Conquistador," p. 91). As with Edgeworth, the mother in the text is not necessarily wholly coterminous with the mothering presence who creates the tale. In "The Heroine as Her Author's Daughter," *Feminist Criticism: Essays on Theory, Poetry, and Prose*, ed. Cheryl L. Brown and Karen Olson (Metuchen, New Jersey and London: Scarecrow Press, 1978), pp. 244–53, and in "On Female Identity and Writing by Women," *Writing and Sexual Difference*, ed. Elizabeth Abel (Chicago and London: University of Chicago Press, 1982), pp. 177–92, Judith Kegan Gardiner argues that in some modern women's novels, the heroine is her author's daughter; I would extend her insight to embrace the whole of a story for juveniles as a narrative space encoding a wish for remothering.

14   "To the Reader," *Patronage*; Miss [Anne Isabella] Thackeray (Mrs. Richmond Ritchie), *A Book of Sibyls: Mrs. Barbauld, Miss Edgeworth, Mrs. Opie, Miss Austen* (London: Smith, Elder, 1883), p. 92; *Memoir*, 1:96; *Helen: A Tale*, 3 vols. (London: Richard Bentley, 1834). John Preston, "The Lost World of Maria Edgeworth" (review essay), *Essays in Criticism* 24 (April 1974): 198–207, briefly but perceptively remarks on Edgeworth's penchant for family themes.

15   Quoted in Rowland Grey, "Maria Edgeworth and Etienne Dumont," *Dublin Review* 145 (1909): 255, 257; [Roland E. Prothero], "The Novels of Maria Edgeworth" (review essay), *Quarterly Review* 182 (Oct. 1895): 305, 321.

16   Woolf, pp. 101, 79; Gaston Bachelard, *The Poetics of Space*, trans. Maria Jolas, 1958 (Boston: Beacon, 1969), p. 159. For an overview of the tradition to which Edgeworth belongs, see my "Impeccable Governesses, Rational Dames, and Moral Mothers: Mary Wollstonecraft and the Female Tradition in Georgian Children's Books," *Children's Literature*, ed. Margaret Higonnet and Barbara Rosen (New Haven and London: Yale University Press, 1986), 14:31–59. By the close of the 1840s, Edgeworth had lived to see her adult reputation rather faded, but her tales for the young were reprinted into this century, and the vividly depicted youngsters who people her stories evidence her claim to be considered the founder of the realistic nursery novel. Published the year before her death, *Orlandino* (Edinburgh: William and Robert Chamber, 1848) demonstrates her continuing liveliness.

17 Edgeworth's note is prefixed to the second edition of *Patronage* (1814); the title of Rachel M. Brownstein, *Becoming A Heroine: Reading About Women in Novels* (New York: Viking, 1982), encodes a whole mythology; Jacqueline Rose, *The Case of Peter Pan, or The Impossibility of Children's Fiction* (London and Basingstoke: Macmillan, 1984), p. 1; Rogers is quoted in Henry Crabb Robinson, *Henry Crabb Robinson on Books and Their Writers*, ed. Edith J. Morley, 3 vols. (London: J. M. Dent, 1938), 1:436 (6 Jan. 1834).

18 Edgeworth is quoted in H. W. Häusermann, *The Genevese Background: Studies of Shelley, Francis Danby, Maria Edgeworth, Ruskin, Meredith, and Joseph Conrad in Geneva (With Hitherto Unpublished Letters)* (London: Routledge and Kegan Paul, 1952), p. 81; *Memoir*, 1:84, 73. Partly to accommodate the audience, many early children's books are as miniature as their readers, but such self-conscious shrinkage is also one of the eighteenth-century's most popular tropes, a way to contain and make sense of the world, as indicated in the survey of Philip Stevick, "Miniaturization in Eighteenth-Century English Literature," *University of Toronto Quarterly* 38 (Jan. 1969): 159–73. The miniature, Bachelard remarks, "allows us to be world conscious at slight risk" (p. 161). Edgeworth knew her natural talent was for bounded delineations of domestic life and worried to Mrs. Barbauld over her longest and probably worst novel, *Patronage*: "It is so vast a subject that it flounders about in my hands and overpowers me," in Anna Letitia Le Breton, ed., *Memoir of Mrs. Barbauld, Including Letters and Notices of Her Family and Friends* (London: George Bell and Sons, 1874), p. 149. [Francis Jeffrey], Review of *Tales of Fashionable Life*, by Maria Edgeworth, *Edinburgh Review* 14 (July 1809): 380, 376; the description of Maria's aim is Richard Lovell Edgeworth's, *Tales of Fashionable Life*, 1809, 1:v.

19 Extravagant references to Honora abound throughout the following works by Anna Seward: *The Poetical Works of Anna Seward: With Extracts from Her Literary Correspondence*, ed. Walter Scott, 3 vols. (Edinburgh: John Ballantyne; London: Longman, Hurst, Rees, and Orme, 1810); *Letters of Anna Seward*, 6 vols. (Edinburgh: Archibald Constable; London: Longman, Hurst, Rees, Orme, and Brown, William Miller, and John Murray, 1811); *Memoirs of the Life of Dr. Darwin, Chiefly During His Residence at Lichfield, with Anecdotes of His Friends, and Criticisms of His Writings* (London: J. Johnson, 1804). Seward's *Monody on Major André* [sic]: *To Which Are Added Letters Addressed to Her by Major André in the Year 1769*, 2nd ed. (Lichfield: J. Jackson; London: Robinson, Cadell and Evans; Oxford: Prince; Cambridge: Merrill; Bath: Pratt and Clinch, 1781), prints letters by another of Honora's admirers, the John André who won fame by being executed as a British spy in the Benedict Arnold affair. Seward seems never to have forgiven Richard Lovell for taking Honora away, since "Honora was her darling (sister, husband, and child combined)," p. 48, in Margaret Ashmun, *The Singing Swan: An Account of Anna Seward and Her Acquaintance with Dr. Johnson, Boswell, and Others of Their Time*, 1931 (New York: Greenwood, 1968), which discusses the relationship throughout. Another rejected suitor was Richard

Lovell's best friend, the eccentric educator Thomas Day; the entry for
Seward in Janet Todd, ed., *A Dictionary of British and American Women Writers
1660–1800* (Totowa, New Jersey: Rowman and Allanheld, 1985), p. 281,
grotesquely conflates Honora with the two young girls whom Day brought
up as an educational experiment.

20   *Memoir,* 1:3; for the new maternal ideal, see Ruth Bloch, "American Feminine Ideals in Transition: The Rise of the Moral Mother," *Feminist Studies* 4
(June 1978): 101–26; Nancy Cott, "Notes Toward an Interpretation of
Antebellum Childrearing," *Psychohistory Review* 6 (Spring 1978): 4–20; and
my "Impeccable Governesses."

21   For Honora's authorship and the intellectual background of the educational
experiment, see Richard Lovell Edgeworth and Maria Edgeworth, *Memoirs
of Richard Lovell Edgeworth, Esq.: Begun by Himself and Concluded by his Daughter,
Maria Edgeworth,* 1820, 2 vols. in 1 (Boston: Wells and Lilly, 1821), 2:67,
103, 187–88; Butler, pp. 61–65; Christina Edgeworth Colvin and Charles
Morgenstern, "The Edgeworths: Some Early Educational Books," *Book Col-
lector* 26 (Spring 1977): 40; Maria Edgeworth and Richard Lovell Edgeworth, *Practical Education,* 2 vols. in 1 (London: Joseph Johnson, 1798),
733–34. The quotation from the story is from [Honora Edgeworth], *Practical
Education: or, The History of Harry and Lucy,* vol. 2 (Lichfield: Printed by J.
Jackson and sold by J. Johnson, London, 1780), p. iv. No previous volume
is known; it was printed, but not officially published. Somewhat confusingly, the very rare little book's title was picked up in later publications — the
1798 educational treatise and the Harry and Lucy stories which were part of
Early Lessons (1801), *Continuation of Early Lessons* (1814), and *Harry and Lucy
Concluded: Being the Last Part of Early Lessons,* 4 vols. (London: R. Hunter,
and Baldwin, Cradock, and Joy, 1825). Maria carefully revised the 1780
story when she reprinted it in *Early Lessons.* The 1780 story's preface, pp. vii–
viii, praises "the ingenious Mrs. Barbould" (sic) for her "lessons far superior
to any, that have hitherto been written"; a notebook on Barbauld's work and
a draft letter to the author document her influence, as do the comments on
books in the 1798 *Practical Education* (unpublished material is cited in Butler,
pp. 51, 61). Noting only the 1798 treatise's suggestions for improvement,
the authoritative Osborne catalogue obscures female affiliations by mislead-
ingly remarking that Barbauld's "effort was criticized by the Edgeworths,"
The Osborne Collection of Early Children's Books, 1566–1910: A Catalogue, ed.
Judith St. John, 1958, 1975, 2 vols. (Toronto: Toronto Public Library,
1975), 1:108. Anna Laetitia Barbauld's pioneering work was printed anony-
mously as *Lessons for Children in Four Parts,* 1778–79 (London: J. Johnson,
1808). Baillie is quoted in Wilfred Partington, ed., *The Private Letter-Books of
Sir Walter Scott* (New York: Frederick A. Stokes, 1930), p. 263; Maria's
evaluation of her father in Edgeworth and Edgeworth, *Memoirs,* 2:4, 198,
appears over and over in similar terms throughout her correspondence.

22   Richard Lovell's letters are quoted in Butler, p. 56, and *Memoir,* 1:6–7.
Rosamond: A Sequel, 1:v. The 1811 letter Butler quotes, p. 477, refers to "my

father who says the defect of my character is an inordinate desire to be beloved," and Richard Lovell's 1817 deathbed injunctions reiterate the same motif. Maria writes that "his last exhortation was against the indulgence of weak and vain sensibility . . . the defect of my disposition," quoted in Grey, p. 260. And family records similarly note the father's worry that, misled by imaginative sympathy, the generous and impulsive Maria might squander her livelihood; interestingly, however, the father characterized his daughter Fanny, Maria's passionately loved special daughter among all the children, as "prudence itself," Harriet Jessie Butler and Harold Edgeworth Butler, eds., *The Black Book of Edgeworthstown and Other Edgeworth Memories 1585-1817* (London: Faber and Gwyer, 1927), pp. 209-10. Ironically, it was the supposedly imprudent Maria who methodically resurrected the family fortunes after her brother Lovell involved the estate in serious financial difficulties. In her final adult novel, Maria has her maternal authority figure criticize one of her paired heroines for "this inordinate desire to be loved, this impatience of not being loved," *Helen*, 1:67. Marilyn Butler argues that only in this late work does Maria weigh youthful sensibilities against judgmental adult virtues to the advantage of the former, but close study of Edgeworth's whole juvenile corpus suggests a more complex, long-lived pattern.

23 *Memoir*, 1:7, 3, 8; Edgeworth and Edgeworth, *Memoirs*, 1:108. The autobiographical portions of the *Memoirs* dealing with Honora are resonant with feeling as Richard Lovell's usually terse and antiromantic prose is not; he insisted that she was the "most beloved as a wife, a sister, and a friend, of any person I have ever known. Each of her own family, unanimously, almost naturally, preferred her. . . . All her friends adored her, if treating her with uniform deference and veneration may be called adoring" (1:169). Visiting England over thirty years after her death, he stopped the chaise to walk to her monumental stone; given Honora's penchant for instilling "habits of exactness and order" in her young stepdaughter, it seems fitting that Maria records, "The white marble is perfectly fresh," Edgeworth and Edgeworth, *Memoirs*, 1:169; *Letters from England, 1813-1844*, ed. Christina Colvin (Oxford: Clarendon Press, 1971), p. 21. The Edgeworth papers abound in testimonies to her unusual strength of character. When Frances married Richard Lovell in 1798, for example, she seems to have worried less over taking the place of her immediate predecessor, Elizabeth (Honora's sister), than a "memory . . . of traditional power over the imagination . . . of one highly gifted and graced with every personal and mental endowment — the more than *celebrated*, the revered Honora," Edgeworth and Edgeworth, *Memoirs*, 2:113. The very stateliness of Maria's phrasing suggests her hidden reservations and contrasts sharply with her many playfully affectionate, even childish notes to Frances, e.g., *Memoir*, 3:194, signed "your old petted nursling."

24 HM 28502, letter to Fanny Robinson, Huntington Library manuscript; I am grateful to the Library for permission to quote from these documents.

Edgeworth's account of her art is in *Memoir*, 3:144–60. The late letter from *Memoir*, 3:194, is typical of many others.

25 HM 28587; HM 28590; HM 28588; HM 28589; the description of Edgeworth as novelist is quoted in Edgar MacDonald, p. 31.

26 P. H. Newby, *Maria Edgeworth*, English Novelists Series (London: Arthur Barker, 1950), p. 28; Butler, pp. 477, 427. Philippe Ariès, *Centuries of Childhood: A Social History of Family Life*, trans. Robert Baldick, 1960 (New York: Vintage, 1962), fathered the current industry of family history research.

27 Susan Stewart, *On Longing: Narratives of the Miniature, the Gigantic, the Souvenir, the Collection* (Baltimore and London: Johns Hopkins University Press, 1984), p. xii; Bachelard, pp. 161, 150; *Rosamond: A Sequel*, 1:iv.

28 James Boaden, ed., *Memoirs of Mrs. Inchbald: Including Her Familiar Correspondence with the Most Distinguished Persons of Her Time*, 2 vols. (London: Richard Bentley, 1833), 2:197; *Memoir*, 2:11, 279, 257.

29 *Memoir*, 3:265, 267; quoted in Grey, p. 255.

"THE LANGUAGE OF REAL FEELING": INTERNAL SPEECH IN THE JANE AUSTEN NOVEL

John A. Dussinger

IN CHARLOTTE Smith's *Rural Walks* (1795), the all-knowing mentor, Mrs. Woodfield, attempts to defend the novels of Richardson against the objections of the young Caroline, who finds them old-fashioned, and not simply because Sir Charles Grandison wears a wig: "I find you are minutely well read in these books, and you therefore must know, that, with all those faults of tediousness and repetition, they contain characters very strongly discriminated, and lessons of the purest morality."[1] What is remarkable here is the consciousness that Richardson and other novelists of the mid-century are technically flawed and obsolete. It is a hindsight parallel to Wordsworth's regarding the eighteenth-century poetic diction and mirrors his aim of rendering "common life . . . as far as was possible, in a selection of language really used by men."[2] At issue is whether writing can appropriate the content and manner of ordinary speech, and if so, by what means.

Rather than imitate regional and class dialect as in Scott's novels, Jane Austen's speech-based prose does something more subtle in its "selection of language really used by men": it incorporates the "tediousness and repetition" of everyday discourse within a narrative economy that in effect makes a boring subject interesting. To this end, Austen found the means of closing the gap between narrator and character by merging description with various codes of represented speech, resulting in the phenomenon of free indirect discourse (FID), which was first identified by Swiss, German, and French philologists in the late nineteenth century, and usually termed *die erlebte Rede* or *le style indirect libre*.[3]

Basically, free indirect discourse is a hybrid form of direct discourse (DD) and indirect discourse (ID). Like ID it transposes the present verb tense of DD to the past and changes the pronoun from first to third person:

"I *am* glad."   He said that *he was* glad.

Like DD it is syntactically independent and is even more isolated than a quotation. For our purposes, the most important feature is the transposition from DD of affective language to imply the speaker's attitude, which is normally eliminated in ID:

"Oh! I am glad."   Oh! He was glad.

As a third form of speech presentation, FID opens up a variety of narrative distancing in contrast to the more orthodox forms of DD and ID.[4]

Through the technique of FID, Austen's parodic text allows fragments of a character's speech to blend indiscriminately with the narrator's "authoritative" voice:

> and they were still discussing the point, when Mr. Knightley, who had left the room immediately after his brother's first report of the snow, came back again, and told them that he had been out of doors to examine, and could answer for there not being the smallest difficulty in their getting home, whenever they liked it, either now or an hour hence. *He had gone beyond the sweep — some way along the Highbury road — the snow was no where above half an inch deep — in many places hardly enough to whiten the ground; a very few flakes were falling at present, but the clouds were parting, and there was every appearance of its being soon over. He had seen the coachmen, and they both agreed with him in there being nothing to apprehend.* (E, pp. 127–28)[5]

Introduced by conventional ID ("Mr. Knightley . . . told them that he had been out of doors . . ."), the subsequent FID passage not only compresses the details needed to defuse the situation but also replicates the hero's calm disinterestedness, evidenced in his exact measurement of the snowfall, in contrast to the previous witnesses who had axes to grind.

Abbreviating a report to emphasize the speaker's "selection of language" is an important means of characterization, which requires some method of repetition — and if possible, without tediousness. Austen's narrative often moves quickly from an Olympian perspective to an individual's idiosyncratic stance:

> The Miss Bertrams' admiration of Mr. Crawford was more rapturous than any thing which Miss Crawford's habits made her likely to feel. [*Gener-*

alization based on the different social backgrounds of the women involved] She acknowledged, however, that the Mr. Bertrams were very fine young men, that two such young men were not often seen together even in London, and that their manners, particularly those of the eldest, were very good. [*An individual attitude registered by ID*] *He* had been much in London, and had more liveliness and gallantry than Edmund, and must, therefore, be preferred; and, indeed, his being the eldest was another strong claim. She had felt an early presentiment that she *should* like the eldest best. She knew it was her way. [*The attitude expanded by FID*] (MP, p. 47)

In a movement from general to particular, from the narrator's voice to the character's, the whole passage renders Mary Crawford's character by way of reporting her preference for Tom Bertram's "manners," and then as if secondarily, for his being heir to the estate.

A major effect of FID is the illusion of depth to character. In his germinal work of the 1920s, translated as *Marxism and the Philosophy of Language*, Mikhail Mikhailovich Bakhtin (using the pseudonym V. N. Volosinov) attributes the individual personality to a theme of language. Rather than something prior to and detachable from words, selfhood is essentially verbal repetition within a dialogical field — *heteroglossia*, which involves narrative and dialogue in an ideological matrix.[6] As Bakhtin shows, the technique of FID is crucial to projecting the requisite interiority of the self; and though not mentioning Austen's novels in particular, he stresses the polyvocal text of comic fiction in general.[7] Perhaps most essential to *heteroglossia* is the way verbal clusters become associated with an identity, which in turn may be referred to and imitated within the text. Narrative language gains significance by its parodic allusiveness, that is, by its sense of an "inner," primary, and "outer," secondary space.

Austen sometimes uses description as a subterfuge, suppressing "actual speech" while giving the barest key terms for a character's presence:

This topic was discussed very happily, and others succeeded of similar moment, and passed away with similar harmony; but the evening did not close without a little return of *agitation*. The *gruel* came and supplied a great deal to be said — *much praise* and many comments — undoubting decision of *its wholesomeness for every constitution*, and pretty severe Philippics upon the many houses where it was never met with *tolerable*; — but, unfortunately, among the failures which the daughter had to instance, the most recent, and therefore most prominent, was in her own cook at South End, a young woman hired for the time, who never had been able to understand what she meant by *a basin of nice smooth gruel, thin, but not too thin*. Often as she had wished for and ordered it, she had never been able to get any thing *tolerable*. Here was a dangerous opening. (E, pp 104–05, my emphasis)

Until the middle of this passage ("the failures which the daughter had to instance") the report avoids identifying any speaker at all but instead focuses on how the physical object—the gruel—prompts nervous responses with embedded ideologies, the vocal proponents dominating over the quiescent dissenters. Obviously the speaker herself has no opinions of her own to express but essentially simulates her father's in order to humor him and if possible to stave off any attack from her increasingly annoyed husband. Although the conversation is ostensibly about gruel, the real issue, we discover fully by the end of the chapter, is whether the hypochondriacal father can uphold his will over his daughters and ally them against his male rivals. Yet Mr. Woodhouse is never mentioned by name as in a conventional report; instead, the motif of the gruel implies not only the character's idiosyncrasies but the whole spectrum of fears in the *heteroglossia* concerning emergence from the womb and survival in a competitive adult society. In this remarkable instance, not even the third person pronoun of FID appears since Mr. Woodhouse's associations with gruel (pp. 24, 100-1) have become too well established by this time to need emphasis.

During the past half century numerous attempts to describe Austen's language have noted, mostly in passing, the importance of FID to her "psychological realism"; but in a monograph almost wholly overlooked, Willi Bühler provided the first full-scale analysis of this narrative strategy in her novels.[8] On the principle that the text is a dynamic interaction between author, character, and reader, he posits the idea that the merest report of a speech can receive some coloring of experience, an idea remarkably similar to Bakhtin's dialogicity.[9]

Among the high points of Austen's use of FID are those scenes where some vital information is communicated after a period of increasing tension and doubt:

> He had found her agitated and low. —*Frank Churchill was a villain.*— He heard her declare that she had never loved him. *Frank Churchill's character was not desperate.* —*She was his own Emma*, by hand and word, when they returned into the house; and if he could have thought of Frank Churchill then, he might have deemed him a very good sort of fellow. (E, p. 433)

This passage reveals the complex distancing effects possible in Austen's narrative. The underscored clauses indicate the usual FID reporting, and if transposed to ID could be introduced as follows:

> Mr. Knightley felt that *Frank Churchill was a villain.*
> Mr. Knightley felt that *Frank Churchill's character was not desperate.*
> Mr. Knightley felt that *she was his own Emma.*

The dullness of repeating the introductory formula is perhaps enough reason to justify the shortcut taken by FID here; but clearly it is the antithesis between simple declaration of fact and the hero's immediate response that represents the very rhythm of desire. In contrast to these closeups, the last conditional and main clauses, it will be noticed, imply a narrator's distant perspective, with the question of what Mr. Knightley was in fact thinking at this moment left unanswered. This fadeout suggests the last temporal instant in the scene, the story's "present time"; but from the context of previous paragraphs that give a shorthand account of the lovers' confessions, we can see yet another temporal frame enclosing the statements of fact, which subordinates Mr. Knightley's process of reconciliation with his enemy to Emma's point of view. A transposition would reveal this frame as follows:

> When Mr. Knightley found me agitated and low he regarded Frank Churchill a villain. But when he heard me say that I had never loved him he felt reconciled toward his imagined rival. When we returned into the house he took my hand and said: "You are my own Emma."

Note that the last part of the original sentence cannot be converted to the first person since it belongs to the distant narrator rather than to Emma. It is this flexible handling of point of view that Austen achieves through FID.

In pursuing the sense of FID as "erlebte Rede," that is, "experienced speech," Bühler offers a loose mixture of philological and phenomenological categories. At the outset, however, he does not take into account sufficiently the important changes in printing conventions for representing "actual speech" in the early novel. As Vivienne Mylne has shown, in both eighteenth-century French and English prose typographical marks for dialogue, when used at all, were far from standardized. Sometimes italics were used to indicate such irregular speech as Friday's broken English in *Robinson Crusoe*; but beginning in the 1740s, dialogue tended to be set off by a combination of dashes and inverted commas.[10]

Thus until about the time of Dickens quotation marks could be used for reported as well as direct speech, and it is possible that the conscious application of FID occurred as a by-product of the effort toward typographical standardization. Private thoughts often have the same status as dialogue in Austen's text, but even this dichotomy may soften in the grey area of reported speech:

> "You will stay, I am sure; you will stay and nurse her;" cried he, turning to her and speaking with a glow, and yet a gentleness, which seemed almost restoring the past. She coloured deeply; and he recollected himself, and

moved away. — She expressed herself most willing, ready, happy to remain. *"It was what she had been thinking of, and wishing to be allowed to do. — A bed on the floor in Louisa's room would be sufficient for her, if Mrs. Harville would but think so."* (P, p. 114)

As if deliberately to overthrow the limitations of DD and ID, Anne Elliot is both thinking and talking in this scene. This typographical indirectness, however, is a legacy of the eighteenth-century novelist's ideal of "writing-to-the-moment":

> With this view he gave himself airs very early;
> 'That his Grandfather and Uncles were his Stewards:
> 'That no man ever had better: That Daughters were
> 'but incumbrances and drawbacks upon a family:'
> And *this* low and familiar expression was often in his
> mouth, and uttered always with the self-complaisance
> which an imagined happy thought can be supposed to
> give the speaker. . . .[11]

Thanks to the relative fluidity of the printed page in his day, Sterne experimented with a variety of typographical indicators for reported speech and used quotation marks infrequently for direct or indirect discourse:

> — the Marquis de B**** wish'd to have it thought the affair was somewhere else than in his brain. "He could like to take a trip to England," and ask'd much of the English ladies. Stay where you are, I beseech you, Mons. le Marquise, said I — Les Messrs. Angloise can scarce get a kind look from them as it is. — The marquis invited me to supper.[12]

To some extent, it appears that FID came about as an accident just at a time when lexicography, grammar, pronunciation, penmanship, and other linguistic disciplines, printing included, fell under the sway of "correctness."[13] Yet, even if we allow for precedents in other writers before her, Austen stands out clearly as a conscious innovator with this narrative indirectness.

Although the distinction is not easy to maintain, Bühler sees FID as an imitation of speech, on the one hand, and as a transcript of thought, on the other. In his opinion, Austen employs FID with such playfulness that it is almost as if she wants to make up for the lost time before its invention.[14] The readerly illusion promoted by reported speech is the disclosure of character through some rhetorical peculiarity:

He saw no fault in the room, he would acknowledge none which they suggested. *No, it was long enough, broad enough, handsome enough. It would hold the very number for comfort. They ought to have balls there at least every fortnight through the winter. Why had not Miss Woodhouse revived the former good old days of the room? — She who could do any thing in Highbury!* (E, p. 198)

After the narrator's brief statement about the character, the negative exclamation signals the shift to FID and calls forth the "experienced" voice of the "practised politician." In this context, however, except for Mr. Knightley's prejudiced attitude, the reader is on his own in siding with the pro-ball or anti-ball factions; and whatever moral opprobrium owing to Frank Churchill, the interloper does perform a service in bringing life to a stagnant community.

When dialogue comprises an automatic interplay of questions and answers, FID is especially effective in sketching just a few details of a verbal encounter:

Her enquiries after her sister were not very favourably answered. *Miss Bennet had slept ill, and though up, was very feverish and not well enough to leave her room.* (PP, p. 33)

In another example, various forms of indirectness compete in rendering a polite exchange:

Miss Tilney added her own wishes. *Catherine was greatly obliged; but it was quite out of her power. Mr. and Mrs. Allen would expect her back every moment.* The general declared he could say no more; the claims of Mr. and Mrs. Allen were not to be superseded; but on some other day he trusted, when longer notice could be given, they would not refuse to spare her to her friend. *"Oh, no; Catherine was sure they would not have the least objection, and she should have great pleasure in coming."* (NA, p. 103)

As will be discussed shortly, while cutting through the verbiage usual in such situations, FID almost inevitably enhances the "inner" self as something apart from the "outer" self presented in speech. Drawn to Henry Tilney, Catherine, we know, wants very much to accept their invitation here but sets duty over love.

Besides the advantages of proportioning narrative and dialogue economically, FID imitates the very movement of conversation, capturing significant pauses that imply evasive behavior, shyness, or simply shortness of breath. The adult prodding the child to talk is a remarkable instance:

"My dear little cousin," said he with all the gentleness of an excellent nature, "what can be the matter?" And sitting down by her, was at great pains to overcome her shame in being so surprised, and persuade her to speak openly. *"Was she ill? or was any body angry with her? or had she quarrelled with Maria and Julia? or was she puzzled about any thing in her lessons that he could explain? Did she, in short, want any thing he could possibly get her, or do for her?"* For a long while no answer could be obtained beyond a "no, no — not at all — no, thank you;" but he still persevered. (MP, p. 15)

Or the confusion of voices during an emergency:

Charles, Henrietta, and Captain Wentworth were the three in consulta-tion, and for a little while it was only an interchange of perplexity and terror. *"Uppercross, — the necessity of some one's going to Uppercross, — the news to be conveyed — how it could be broken to Mr. and Mrs. Musgrove — the lateness of the morning, — an hour already gone since they ought to have been off, — the impossibility of being in tolerable time.* At first, they were capable of nothing more to the purpose than such exclamations; but, after a while, Captain Wentworth, exerting himself, said. . . ." (P, p. 113)

Just as in music, dance, stage acting, oratory, and any kind of public speaking interruptions in sound are powerfully expressive — for instance, the abrupt silence at the end of a phrase in a Beethoven symphony — so in narrative the unsaid holds import, often throwing into relief the banality of the word; and FID is a means to this end in Austen's novels.

After demonstrating a variety of imitated speech, Bühler concludes with Austen's representation of thought per se; and although the distinc-tion is useful for separating the "inner" and "outer" frames of reference, in contrast to later nineteenth-century writers there is really no interest here in a language to convey psychic experience. In spite of her dazzling inventiveness in FID, Austen, according to Roy Pascal, has two blind spots: (1) while replicating her characters' thoughts she omits the physi-cal scene — the whole spatial surroundings, the appearance of the other persons in the room, and other visual and auditory data — that enters into those thoughts; and (2) she renders mental life only in grammatical sentences, including the sentence fragments that indicate extreme emo-tional states; the pre-conscious stages of thought do not interest her. Adopting the tory view, Pascal attributes these shortcomings to the author's rationalism and possible dread of probing very deeply into the heart.[15] Even if we allow these limitations in Austen's "psychological realism," Bühler's analysis calls attention to narrative methods used that give an intriguing depth to the "inner" life of her characters.

Bühler sees two categories of FID at work in representing the mind:

erlebte Reflexion ("experienced reflection"), where the thoughts and feelings are in the foreground; and *erlebte Eindruck* ("experienced impression"), where the content itself that causes these thoughts and feelings are in the foreground. In the first case, it is the growth of consciousness, its blending into the inner world of reflection; in the second, it is the outer world that constitutes the whole and yields only a light coloring to the character. In the one kind of perception the mind is active toward the environment; in the other, it is passive.

The following passage illustrates the foregrounding of emotion:

> The hair was curled, and the maid sent away, and Emma sat down to think and be miserable. — *It was a wretched business, indeed! — Such an overthrow of every thing she had been wishing for! — Such a development of every thing most unwelcome! — Such a blow for Harriet! — That was the worst of all.* Every part of it brought pain and humiliation, of some sort or other; but, compared with the evil to Harriet, all was light; and she would gladly have submitted to feel yet more mistaken — *more in error — more disgraced by mis-judgment,* than she actually was, could the effects of her blunders have been confined to herself. (E, p. 134)

After the routine matters of hair curling and maids are over, Emma can at last sit down alone and reflect on all her miscalculations about Mr. Elton. Again, in another context the physical place is mainly the catalyst for reflection: "As for Elizabeth, her thoughts were at Pemberley this evening more than the last; and the evening, though as it passed it seemed long, was not long enough to determine her feelings towards *one* in that mansion; and she lay awake two whole hours, endeavouring to make them out. She certainly did not hate him. No; hatred had vanished long ago, and she had almost as long been ashamed of ever feeling a dislike against him, that could be so called" (PP, p. 265). Her views of Darcy have changed after visiting his family estate, but what occupies her mind here is her unexpressed indebtedness to the owner of that noble mansion: "It was gratitude. — Gratitude, not merely for having once loved her, but for loving her still well enough, to forgive all the petulance and acrimony of her manner in rejecting him, and all the unjust accusations accompanying her rejection." In terminology, if not in narrative style, such instances of FID recall the intricate cases of conscience found in eighteenth-century prose fiction; but except for the epistolary novels the temporal dimension of Austen's represented thought is much more pronounced than in any of her predecessors.[16]

Given the casuistical discourse that prevails in the narrative, instances of "experienced impression" are relatively infrequent. Emma's daydreaming at Ford's is a rare moment of surrender to the environment:

> — Much could not be hoped from the traffic of even the busiest part of Highbury; — Mr. Perry walking hastily by, Mr. William Cox letting himself in at the office door, Mr. Cole's carriage horses returning from exercise, or a stray letter-boy on an obstinate mule, were the liveliest objects she could presume to expect; and when her eyes fell only on the butcher with his tray, a tidy old woman travelling homewards from shop with her full basket, two curs quarrelling over a dirty bone, and a string of dawdling children round the baker's little bow-window eyeing the gingerbread, she knew she had no reason to complain, and was amused enough; quite enough still to stand at the door. A mind lively and at ease, can do with seeing nothing, and can see nothing that does not answer. (E, p. 233)

None of the particulars in this scene have any bearing on Emma's recent debacle with Mr. Elton and her present concern for Harriet's feelings; in fact, the passage is a tour de force, almost as if to demonstrate, contrary to Roy Pascal's criticism, that the means of evoking the perceived physical space are available whenever needed.

A more functional use of "experienced impression" registers the character's awakening simultaneously with her perception of the landscape:

> Elizabeth's mind was too full for conversation, but she saw and admired every remarkable spot and point of view. They gradually ascended for half a mile, and then found themselves at the top of a considerable eminence, where the wood ceased, and the eye was instantly caught by Pemberley House, situated on the opposite side of a valley, into which the road with some abruptness wound. *It was a large, handsome, stone building, standing well on rising ground, and backed by a ridge of high woody hills; — and in front, a stream of some natural importance was swelled into greater, but without any artificial appearance. Its banks were neither formal, nor falsely adorned.* Elizabeth was delighted. She had never seen a place for which nature had done more, or where natural beauty had been so little counteracted by an awkward taste. They were all of them warm in their admiration; and at that moment she felt, that to be mistress of Pemberley might be something! (PP, p. 245)

Once appropriated by FID as Elizabeth's heightened awareness of Mr. Darcy, the building and grounds, apart from their being proof of the owner's good taste, momentarily symbolize masculine power in all its rising and swelling pride; and overwhelmed by this sexual apprehension, she succumbs to a desire hitherto denied and scarcely recovers for the rest of the story.

In another context the "experienced impression" enlivens the character's sense of her world but at first does not alter her beliefs in any way:

> She felt all the honest pride and complacency which her alliance with the present and future proprietor could fairly warrant, as she viewed *the respectable size and style of the building, its suitable, becoming, characteristic situation, low and sheltered — its ample gardens stretching down to meadows washed by a stream, of which the Abbey, with all the old neglect of prospect, had scarcely a sight*. . . .
>
> *It was a sweet view — sweet to the eye and the mind. English verdure, English culture, English comfort, seen under a sun bright, without being oppressive.* (E, pp. 358, 360)

The heroine does not discover anything new about the hero in the perception of this landscape, and the abrupt sight of him together with her young friend only increases the pleasure of the place rather than arouse any jealousy. From "experienced impression" the narrative shifts to "experienced reflection" as Emma contemplates the evident intimacy between the couple before her in this English Eden:

> *Mr. Knightley and Harriet! — it was an odd tête-à-tête*; but she was glad to see it. — *There had been a time when he would have scorned her as a companion, and turned from her with little ceremony. Now they seemed in pleasant conversation.* There had been a time also when Emma would have been sorry to see Harriet in a spot so favourable for the Abbey-Mill Farm; but now she feared it not. *It might be safely viewed with all its appendages of prosperity and beauty, its rich pastures, spreading flocks, orchard in blossom, and light column of smoke ascending.* (E, p. 360)

At this point Emma feels complete trust in Mr. Knightley; and the euphoria from viewing the farm country here depends, of course, upon her unquestioned tie with its proprietor. In general, "experienced impression" occurs in moments of the story when the character is relatively at ease with herself and her environment; thus, not surprisingly, it is "experienced reflection" that takes up most of the FID narrative in the Austen text.

Since FID surrenders to the character a large responsibility in the storytelling process, it calls into question the writer's relation to her text. Austen has usually been regarded as the prototype of narrative as well as moral order in the history of the English novel; yet until recently her experimental daring has been mainly an embarrassment.[17] In the most complete rhetorical analysis of *Emma* to date, Graham Hough identifies five kinds of discourse in the Austen novel: (1) the *authorial voice*, which "occurs in passages (usually reflective, hortatory or gnomic) that stand outside the economy of the narrative, short-circuit it, as it were, and constitute a direct address from author to reader"; (2) *objective narrative*, or "the voice of the narrator," as in the opening paragraphs of *Emma* and in various places throughout the novel especially for setting a scene or explaining circumstances; (3) *colored narrative*, restricted to an individual character's point of view, FID as the imitation of thought; (4) *free indirect style*, used intermittently "in short snatches, without breaking the flow of the narrative," i.e., FID as reported speech; and (5) *direct speech* and *dialogue*. Although dialogue and colored narrative (loosely defined) predominate in the overall text, Hough admits that his categories of objective narrative and free indirect style shade imperceptibly into colored narrative; and so the author's alleged governance over the story depends on segments of unquestionably objective perspective.

Despite the difficulty in separating one kind of discourse from another, Hough upholds a rhetorically closed text: "The very perfection with which Jane Austen controls her linguistic apparatus cuts out the element of indeterminacy, of working things out, that is present in later novels — in Charlotte Brontë and George Eliot, for example."[18] From this conviction it is an easy step to conclude that the author represents the feminine half of the upper bourgeoisie who looked back nostalgically in a revolutionary age to the social and moral calm of the *ancien régime*.

But if the whole interplay of FID in the Austen text is more subversive than Hough and other tory readers will allow, his criterion of "general, abstract, evaluative and formally correct" language for objective narrative is tenuous at best. It may be true that certain passages in Austen, to quote C. S. Lewis, "breathe the air of the *Rambler* and *Idler*"[19]; but the evocation of the Augustan ethos is not primarily to give the reader the "correct" interpretation of events vis-à-vis the character's erroneous judgments. On the contrary, the Johnsonian echoes are usually parodic, a conflation of the "high" and "low" styles to give an ironic edge to mere description, as in Hough's examples:

> The real evils indeed of Emma's situation were the power of having rather too much her own way, and a disposition to think a little too well of herself; these were the disadvantages which threatened alloy to her many enjoyments. (E, p. 5)

> Such was Jane Fairfax's history. She had fallen into good hands, known nothing but kindness from the Campbells, and been given an excellent education. Living constantly with right-minded and well-informed people, her heart and understanding had received every advantage of discipline and culture; and Col. Campbell's residence being in London, every lighter talent had been done full justice to, by the attendance of first-rate masters. Her disposition and abilities were equally worthy of all that friendship could do;

and at eighteen or nineteen she was, as far as such an early age can be qualified for the care of children, fully competent to the office of instruction herself. . . . (E, p. 164)

According to Hough, "The authority of the narrative is reinforced by adopting the common form of decent educated discourse."[20]

But surely the word authority needs inverted commas to account for the tongue-in-cheek voice introducing the "handsome, clever, and rich" Emma in conjunction with the lofty diction of the eighteenth-century moral essay — "best blessings of existence," "real evils," and "[moral] danger." Although the narrator prepares us here for a didactic tale about a selfish girl who needs to be taught a lesson, the actual reading of the novel soon involves "real evils" much more complex than those named in the opening paragraphs. Eventually we even learn the identity of this "objective" narrator who enters the story masked in FID: "I am losing all my bitterness against spoilt children, my dearest Emma. I, who am owing all my happiness to *you*, would not it be horrible ingratitude in me to be severe on them?" (E, p. 461). Despite her meddling with other people's lives, Emma has little control over events and, as it turns out, is hardly "spoilt" by "having rather too much her own way"; and to the end Mr. Knightley does not know her potentially dangerous errors concerning Mr. Elton, Jane Fairfax, and Harriet. Furthermore, a heroine with the jocularity to say near the conclusion, "I always deserve the best treatment, because I never put up with any other" (474), is not an appropriate type for the solemn edification that Hough expects of the story.

At first glance, the description of Jane Fairfax seems on safer ground as objective reporting. The voice here does not appear to evoke any particular character in the story and keeps the distance of a Fieldingesque narrator. But on examining this passage within its larger context we can soon discover an ironic tension beneath the calm surface and an ulterior motive for the elaborate detail concerning this character's qualifications — namely, to press her advantage on the marriage market despite her lack of family and to arouse suspicions of a love-and-friendship conflict.

They continued together with unabated regard however, till the marriage of Miss Campbell, *who by that chance, that luck which so often defies anticipation in matrimonial affairs, giving attraction to what is moderate rather than to what is superior,* engaged the affections of Mr. Dixon, a young man, rich and agreeable, almost as soon as they were acquainted; and *was eligibly and happily settled, while Jane Fairfax had yet her bread to earn.* (E, p. 165)

The italicized words are hardly objective but imply a desire similar to Emma's romantic imaginings of a triangular relationship. Towards the end of the next paragraph the ironic narrator sounds indeed very much like the heroine:

> With the fortitude of a devoted noviciate, she had resolved at one-and-twenty to complete the sacrifice, and retire from all the pleasures of life, of rational intercourse, equal society, peace and hope, to penance and mortification for ever.

This is the quasi-medieval world of Gothic romances, with the usual threat of confinement in a Catholic convent; and the voice is the same that renders Emma's reflections upon the discovery of the secret engagement:

> —In Jane's eyes she had been a rival; and well might any thing she could offer of assistance or regard be repulsed. *An airing in the Hartfield carriage would have been the rack, and arrow-root from the Hartfield storeroom must have been poison.* She understood it all; and as far as her mind could disengage itself from the injustice and selfishness of angry feelings, she acknowledged that Jane Fairfax would have neither elevation nor happiness beyond her desert. (E, p. 403)

The language of "decent educated discourse" returns after these nuggets of FID recall the heroine's Gothic imagination, and the juxtaposition of rival styles alerts us to the contingency of individual attitudes rather than pretend objectivity ("as far as her mind could disengage itself from the injustice and selfishness of angry feelings").

Rhetorical criticism usually underestimates the hybrid forms of novelistic discourse, a problem raised by Hough's curious dismissal of what he calls the authorial voice, illustrated in the following well-known apothegms:

> It is a truth universally acknowledged, that a single man in possession of a good fortune, must be in want of a wife. (PP, p. 3)

> Human nature is so well disposed towards those who are in interesting situations, that a young person, who either marries or dies, is sure of being kindly spoken of. (E, p. 181)

> It may be possible to do without dancing entirely. Instances have been known of young people passing many, many months successively, without being at any ball of any description, and no material injury accrue either to body or mind; —but when a beginning is made—when the felicities of rapid

motion have once been, though slightly, felt — it must be a very heavy set that does not ask for more. (E, p. 247)

Although among the most memorable in Austen's text, such epigrammatic passages are really brief and infrequent. Hough observes: "They tend to establish a footing of agreeable complicity between author and reader; but otherwise they are not important, and I shall say little more of them."[21] Yet these examples are most obviously imitative of the Augustan manner; and if so, how can they be unimportant?

Again, "authorial" voice would more accurately denote the function of such Olympian irony; hence, while it privileges the reader, it also implicates her in the human folly addressed in the story. But more important, it parodies "Johnsonese" to convey the mock heroic situations of a minuscule world remote from the historian's universal gaze. Rather than being only brilliant but decorative asides, the epigrammatic sentences call into question more emphatically than the other voices of the text the whole ideal of authority, objectivity, and wisdom. Despite its formal rhetorical structure, for instance, the famous opening of *Pride and Prejudice* announces an economic motive for marrying that dominates not only Mrs. Bennet's but all the characters' behavior in the story. Hardly a detachable quip, the moral proposition reinforces the ideology expressed in various narrative forms, including FID.

Austen's experimental zest for indirectly representing speech created a comic text with an astounding variety of illusionary effects contributing to a character's "presence" in narrative. It is the parodic incorporation of another's speech that Bakhtin identifies as essential to the novel: "Comic style (of the English sort) is based, therefore, on the stratification of common language and on the possibilities available for isolating from these strata, to one degree or another, one's own intentions, without ever completely merging with them. *It is precisely the diversity of speech, and not the unity of a normative shared language, that is the ground of style.*"[22] Yet, as if fearful that her inventive mimicry risks abrogating the storyteller's authority, readers have insisted on Austen's unity by stressing her classical symmetry at the expense of her diversity.

Thus while praising her stratified language and playful texture, Hough nevertheless distrusts the reflexivity of Austen's narrative art and consequently imposes on it a corrective grid: "When the objective narrative is noticeably intruded upon by the subjectivity of the characters, it is always a sign that the characters are departing from the norm. If they were not their subjectivity would be identical with the narrator's and so undetectable."[23] From the foregoing analysis it should be clear why this abstract principle is untenable in the actual reading of Austen's speech-oriented text. Not only is the dichotomy between subject and object a flexible rhetorical strategy in her storytelling (in the end, Mr. Knightley mocks his own objective "lectures"), but the merging of narrator and character in FID may function best independently of explicit norms (Emma's romantic thoughts of Jane Fairfax as tortured victim).

Finally, after acknowledging that direct discourse comprises a major part of Austen's novels, Hough makes a staggering claim for its consistent determinacy: "I cannot think of a single case in *Emma* (or in Jane Austen in general) where the dialogue does more than enlarge and illustrate, though with incomparable justice and vivacity, positions that the narrator has previously outlined. The dramatic propriety is perfect but it is the adjunct to a narrative judgment not a drama in itself."[24] Fortunately, Austen's polyvocal art is not so rigidly methodical. Though on numerous occasions the dialogue echoes the narrative, and vice versa, there are also moments when a character contributes something wholly new to the text without being anticipated by the narrator. Although few, including the narrator, pay any attention to her words, Miss Bates is full of surprises in the early part of the novel. In general, the talkative characters have speeches that go uninterpreted. Much of the dialogue between Elizabeth and Darcy, furthermore, occurs as spontaneous repartee, free of normative closure. It is in the "empty spaces" of *any* imitated speech act that the reader becomes most aware of the writer at work behind the scenes. In Austen's dialogical world the "authorial" narrator simply does not compete successfully all the time with the other narrators/characters in revealing the illusion that passes for truth: after all, "seldom can it happen that something is not a little disguised, or a little mistaken."

Notes

1 Charlotte Smith, *Rural Walks: In Dialogues. Intended for the Use of Young Persons*, Two Volumes in One (Dublin, 1795), p. 153.

2 William Wordsworth, " 'Preface' to *Lyrical Ballads*," *The Norton Anthology of English Literature*, ed. M. H. Abrams et al., 2 vols., Fourth Edition (New York & London: Norton, 1979), 2:162.

3 See Brian McHale, "Free Indirect Discourse: A Survey of Recent Accounts," *PTL: A Journal for Descriptive Poetics and Theory of Literature* 3 (1978): 249–87. Among the most important studies are the following: W. J. M. Bronzwaer, *Tense in the Novel: An Investigation of Some Potentialities of Linguistic Criticism* (Groningen: Wolters-Noordhoff, 1970); Seymour Chatman, *Story and Discourse: Narrative Structure in Fiction and Film* (Ithaca: Cornell

Univ. Press, 1978); Dorrit Cohn, *Transparent Minds* (Princeton: Princeton Univ. Press, 1978); Roger Fowler, *Linguistics and the Novel* (New York & London: Methuen, 1977); Norman Page, *Speech in the English Novel,* English Language Series No. 8 (London: Longman, 1973); Roy Pascal, *The Dual Voice* (Totowa, N.J. & Manchester: Manchester Univ. Press & Rowman and Littlefield, 1977); Stephen Ullmann, *Style in the French Novel* (Oxford: Blackwell, 1964); and V. N. Volosinov [M. M. Bakhtin], *Marxism and the Philosophy of Language,* trans. Ladislav Matejka & I. R. Titunik (New York & London: Seminar Press, 1973).

4 This narrative technique, dubbed "point of view" by Jamesian critics, is ubiquitous in twentieth-century fiction and especially effective in the modern short story:

> They both wanted the child very much. Yet she could not help feeling afraid. *She had her husband on her hands, a terrible joy to her, and a terrifying burden. The child would occupy her love and attention. And then, what of Maurice? What would he do? If only she could feel that he, too, would be at peace and happy when the child came!* She did so want to luxuriate in a rich, physical satisfaction of maternity. *But the man, what would he do? How could she provide for him, how avert those shattering black moods of his, which destroyed them both?*

D. H. Lawrence, "The Blind Man," *The Complete Short Stories,* 3 vols. (New York and Harmondsworth: Penguin, 1976, rptd. 1983), 1:348.

> *Had he brought the coffee?* She had been waiting all day long for coffee. They had forgot it when they ordered at the store the first day.
> *Gosh, no, he hadn't. Lord, now he'd have to go back. Yes, he would if it killed him.* He thought, though, he had everything else. She reminded him it was only because he didn't drink coffee himself. *If he did he would remember it quick enough. Suppose they ran out of cigarettes?* Then she saw the rope. *What was that for?*

Katherine Anne Porter, "Rope," *The Collected Stories of Katherine Anne Porter* (San Diego, New York, & London: Harcourt Brace Jovanovich, 1969), p. 42.

5 All parenthetical references to Austen's novels are to the third edition by R. W. Chapman, 5 vols. (London: Oxford Univ. Press, 1933, rptd. 1960). The following abbreviations are used: E (*Emma*), MP (*Mansfield Park*), P (*Persuasion*), PP (*Pride and Prejudice*), NA (*Northanger Abbey*).

6 Volosinov argues: "Language lights up the inner personality and its consciousness; language creates them and endows them with intricacy and profundity—it does not work the other way. Personality is itself generated through language, not so much, to be sure, in the abstract forms of language, but rather in the ideological themes of language. Personality, from the standpoint of its inner, subjective content, is a theme of language" (*Marxism and the Philosophy of Language,* p. 153.)

7   See "Discourse in the Novel," *The Dialogic Imagination*, ed. Michael Holquist, trans. Caryl Emerson & Michael Holquist (Austin: Univ. of Texas Press, 1981), pp. 259–422.

8   Willi Bühler, *Die "Erlebte Rede" Im Englischen Roman: Ihre Vorstufen und ihre Ausbildung im Werke Jane Austens*, in *Schweizer Anglistische Arbeiten*, 4. Band (Zürich & Leipzig: Max Niehans, [1936]). For a recent study that follows Bühler without fully acknowledging the debt, see Georgi Papançev, *Interior Monologue (Internal Speech) in Jane Austen's Novels*. Sofia Universitet, Fakultet po Zapadni filologi. Godishnik Annuaire, 67 (1973). Norman Page, *The Language of Jane Austen* (Oxford: Blackwell, 1972), cites Bühler in a note (p. 123), along with L. Glauser, *Die erlebte Rede im englischen Roman des 19. Jahrhunderts* (Zürich, 1948), at the beginning of his discussion but does not use his findings. Surprisingly enough, even German scholars ignore Bühler; see Wolfgang G. Müller, "Gefühlsdarstellung bei Jane Austen," *Sprachkunst* 8 (1977): 85–103. My own discussion, including many of the citations from the novels, adopts loosely Bühler's commentary.

9   Bühler states (p. 85): "Ein Bericht von Rede und Mitteilung kann eine schwache Färbung von Erlebtheit annehmen; bald ist es uns, als hörten wir den Mitteilenden sprechen, dann kann es wieder scheinen, als ob wir das Berichtete durch das Medium des Zuhörers hörten; schwache, kaum wahrnehmbare Lichter überspielen das Ganze und erwecken im Leser eine zwiespältige Empfindung; die Gefühlserlebtheit scheint zwischen dem Autor, der sprechenden und der zuhorchenden Gestalt zu orzillieren." [A report of a speech and communication can receive a weak coloring of experience; as soon as we hear the informer speak, it is as if we hear the report through the medium of the listener. Weak, scarcely perceptible lights play about the whole and awaken in the reader a conflicting feeling; the experience of emotion appears to oscillate between the author, the speaker, and the listening character.]

10 Vivienne Mylne, "The Punctuation of Dialogue in Eighteenth-Century French and English Fiction," *Library*, ser. 6, 1 (1979): 43–61.

11 Samuel Richardson, *Clarissa, or, The History of a Young Lady: Comprehending The Most Important Concerns of Private Life*, 7 vols., Fourth Edition (London, 1751), 1:70–71.

12 Laurence Sterne, *A Sentimental Journey Through France and Italy by Mr. Yorick*, ed. Gardner D. Stout, Jr. (Berkeley & Los Angeles: Univ. of California Press, 1967), p. 262.

13 See Elizabeth L. Eisenstein, *The Printing Press as an Agent of Change: Communications and Cultural Transformations in Early Modern Europe*, 2 vols. (Cambridge: Cambridge Univ. Press, 1979); and the abridgement, *The Printing Revolution in Early Modern Europe* (Cambridge: Cambridge Univ. Press, 1983), esp. pp. 50–63. Walter J. Ong, *Orality and Literacy: The Technologizing of the Word* (London & New York: Methuen, 1982). As Bühler and others have pointed out, eighteenth-century novelists from Richardson to Fanny Burney were tentatively aware of FID but did not seize its potential in the way Austen

did. A recent study of Fielding's practice ignores the effects of typography; see Alfred McDowell, "Fielding's Rendering of Speech in *Joseph Andrews* and *Tom Jones,*" *Language and Style* 6 (1973): 83–96.

14 Bühler, p. 82.

15 Roy Pascal, *The Dual Voice*, pp. 59–60.

16 See G. A. Starr, *Defoe and Casuistry* (Princeton: Princeton Univ. Press, 1971). Starr's pioneering work needs to be applied to the later eighteenth-century novelists. In this direction, see Frederick M. Keener, *The Chain of Becoming: The Philosophical Tale, The Novel, and a Neglected Realism of the Enlightenment: Swift, Montesquieu, Voltaire, Johnson, and Austen* (New York: Columbia Univ. Press, 1983); and Douglas Lane Patey, *Probability and Literary Form: Philosophic Theory and Literary Practice in the Augustan Age* (Cambridge: Cambridge Univ. Press, 1984).

17 Marilyn Butler, for instance, vents her frustration over the indeterminacy of the text: "The trouble with *Pride and Prejudice* is that many readers do not perceive just how critical the author is of Elizabeth's way of thinking," *Jane Austen and the War of Ideas* (Oxford: Clarendon, 1975, rptd. 1976), p. 216.

18 Graham Hough, "Narrative and Dialogue in Jane Austen," *Critical Quarterly* 12 (1970): 222.

19 Hough, "Narrative and Dialogue," p. 208.

20 Hough, "Narrative and Dialogue," p. 207.

21 Hough, "Narrative and Dialogue," p. 204.

22 Bakhtin, "Discourse in the Novel," *The Dialogic Imagination*, p. 301.

23 Hough, "Narrative and Dialogue," p. 221.

24 Hough, "Narrative and Dialogue," p. 217.

THE RECEPTION OF THE GOTHIC
NOVEL IN THE 1790s

David H. Richter

THE PROJECT I have been working at for some time is on literary historiography and the Gothic novel. Its overall thesis is that the kind of history you write of a genre depends in part on the way you look at genres.

First and most commonly, a genre may be conceived as the locus of a large repertory of material conventions, which may be adopted by later authors for entirely different purposes. The result is what used to be called an influence study, and which is now called intertextuality, but the process is familiar enough. In the case of the Gothic, one would, for example, examine the stages through which Horace Walpole's daemonic father, Manfred of Otranto, passed in his metamorphosis into Faulkner's daemonic father, Thomas Sutpen.

Second, a genre may be conceived as an Aristotelian form, where the final cause is held constant, though as the genre evolves new and different material elements are brought and shaped to serve that end. The result of this would be a neo–Aristotelian essay on horror fiction and the changes it has undergone from Radcliffe and Lewis through Le Fanu, Stevenson, Stoker and Wilde, to more recent chillers like those of H. P. Lovecraft and Stephen King.

Third, and most important for this study, a genre might be conceived of as an area of literary space, a niche in the ecology of literature. But just as living organisms evolve, so do genres. When the cultural environment which produced the niche changes, the genre must change with it. Under this hypothesis, the Gothic novel begins in the late eighteenth century in dialectical opposition to two other contemporary fictional forms, the didactic novel and the novel of manners. During the nineteenth century, however, the Gothic assumed other roles in opposition to different mainstream forms. For example, when the mainstream novel,

117

toward the end of the century, turned outward to a broad social canvas, as in *Daniel Deronda*, the Gothic turned inward toward an examination of abnormal psychology, as in *Dr. Jekyll and Mr. Hyde*. Furthermore, the Gothic began to spin subgenres out of itself, which around the end of the nineteenth century acquired definition of their own. *Frankenstein* engendered science fiction as a separate mode of hypothetical probability, while the explained supernatural of Radcliffe's novels gave birth to the mystery novel. Owing to both the shifting of its mainstream competition and its shrinkage due to the extravasation of other popular modes, the Gothic today is relegated to two rather decayed apartments in the house of fiction: the horror tale and the popular romance.

How did all this come about? It is my hypothesis that this shifting of literary niches, including the birth of new genres out of old, cannot be explained in purely formal terms, as the opening and exhausting of structural possibilities. Such changes must have been at least partly the result of a complex interaction between producers and consumers, between authors on the one hand and audiences and publishers on the other. The motor for history, in this version, bears some resemblance to what we find in some of the theoretical ideas about reception and literary history proposed by Hans Robert Jauss of the school of Konstanz.

HANS ROBERT JAUSS AND RECEPTION THEORY

Jauss's most influential work, "Literary History as a Challenge to Literary Theory," was published nearly twenty years ago, though it is only beginning to acquire practical influence on the way literary history is conceived and written. Briefly, Jauss's reader-oriented theory, based on the hermeneutics of Hans-Georg Gadamer, views the text in terms of the running dialogue between the newly published work of literature and the audience. Any audience responds to a text in terms of a "horizon of expectations" built up from its previous experience with classic and contemporary literature, as well as its experience of the real world outside literature. The new work may merely fall nicely within the horizon of expectations and be accepted as a simple consumer-good; or it may challenge that horizon. Works that challenge the audience may succeed in altering the way the audience responds to literature, or may fail to do so, and be rejected. Rejected or misunderstood works, however, may succeed in entering the canon later when the literary horizon has, in effect, caught up with them. Similarly, the significance of literary works changes to successive audiences with the change in horizons of expectation. Jauss wants to base the history of literature upon this pattern of interaction between artist and work and audience.[1]

Although Jauss has been accused of merely resuscitating the history of taste[2], he is talking about something far more inclusive. When he talks about the changing "horizons of expectation" of the audience, he is speaking of a history of all the various preconceptions — about art, reading, and the cultural milieu in general — which audiences bring to literary texts.

In examining an audience's responses, the key ingredient is a historical understanding of what Jauss calls "aesthetic experience" — that inventory of the ways people respond to art. Jauss distinguishes between three modes of artistic enjoyment, which he calls *poiesis, aisthesis,* and *catharsis*. The first, *poiesis,* is the experience of art as a productive activity. Once the exclusive preserve of the artist, *poiesis* is shared by the authors of recent open texts with their readers, who must complete their creations. One example is the sense of creativity we experience in helping James evoke the world of *The Golden Bowl.* The second, *aisthesis,* involves the contemplative, passively receptive experience of art. This receptivity can take several forms. One form, which Jauss calls "language-critical," involves a kind of rapturous aporia — what Roland Barthes termed *jouissance* — which is stimulated, say, by Robbe-Grillet's waste land of signifiers. Or it may take what Jauss suggests is the less alienating "cosmological" form when we see the world through another's eyes, as in Proust's *The Past Recaptured.* The third, *catharsis,* is the communicative function of poetry, what brings about in the reader "both a change in belief and the liberation of his mind." This is the familiar "delight and instruct" function of art, which Jauss traces from Aristotle to Brecht. For Jauss, I must stress these three forms of aesthetic experience are not static categories but dialectical alternatives each of which has had its own historical development.[3] The shifting of the audience's motivation for reading from one of these alternatives to another is one of the chief causes of literary change.

One of the virtues of Jauss's reception theory is that it avoids the equal and opposite distortions of Formalist and Marxist versions of literary history. For a Russian Formalist like Yuri Tynjanov, literary history is almost purely intrinsic, and genres grow as artists create space for originality and variation, and decline as this space is progressively exhausted. For a Marxist like Raymond Williams, literary history is almost purely extrinsic, as changes in literature — part of the ideological superstructure of a society — are necessarily tied to social and economic changes occurring in the base. Jauss may seem to stand on the Formalist side of this debate — especially as his critical debates have been principally with the Marxists across the border in East Germany. But his theory straddles this unproductive dilemma: it insists that the history of literature is influenced by changes within society, but that literature nevertheless enjoys a high degree of autonomy, and develops at least in part through avenues of its own design.

One of the characteristic problems raised by Jauss's system is identifying the reader whose shifting interests and psychology are the principal causes of historical change. In reading Jauss one must be aware that "reader" is a potentially ambiguous word. For instance, there is an ideal reader immanent in each text—the so-called "implied reader" of Jauss's colleague at Konstanz, Wolfgang Iser. Yet there are real readers, contemporary with the author or later, whose characteristics may or may not be identical with those the author projected onto his text. In the case of successful popular literature, the distinction between the contemporary audience and the implied reader may be one without a difference. But important books help to mold and shape the audience just as much as the audience shapes the literary canon, and many a novelist—such as Flaubert and Joyce—has written for an implied audience that did not fully come into being until well after his death.

Furthermore, for Jauss reading occurs not in the mass but in different *strata* of the audience, and he discusses reception on three levels: (1) a *Gipfelsebene* of readers who are also creative writers that contribute directly to production: (2) a *mittlere Ebene* of writers who influence the general public but are not directly involved in creativity (e.g., reviewers); (3) and a *präreflexive Ebene* of general readers who merely consume texts—and provide the potential market for their production.[4]

From all this, one would expect that Jauss's practical criticism would consist of studies of the real audience's reaction to various texts at various times throughout history. If so, we would be disappointed. Jauss had been vague in *Literary History as Challenge* about whether the prior commitment of the historian of reception was to the ideal reader immanent in the text or to the real reader who spent real money to acquire the book. But it became clear by the late 1970s that for Jauss the fact that "it is easier to grasp the implied rather than the explicit reader's role" meant that "the role of the implied reader deserves methodological preference."[5] In fact Jauss's preference for the implicit over the explicit reader is not merely a hermeneutical priority. A survey of Jauss's own practical criticism suggests that he is less than enthusiastic about examining, in the messy and difficult ways such historical research requires, how actual readers have responded to texts. Though he gives plenty of lip service to the need to broaden the notion of reading, Jauss has published no examples of the pragmatic influence of the second and third levels of the audience. Instead he prefers to study the authors on the peak reading each other.[6]

One could apply that method to the Gothic without much difficulty. One could create a reception-study concentrating on how Matthew Lewis excitedly read Radcliffe's *Udolpho* and produced *The Monk*, or how Radcliffe read *The Monk*, was horrified in both senses of the word, and retorted with *The Italian*. But such a result is not going to differ very much from old fashioned influence studies. What makes Jauss worth taking up is not any greater precision of terminology that he might lend to influence studies, but rather his implicit notion that literature changes at least in part from the bottom up. The study that follows, an investigation of the reception of the Gothic novel in the decade from 1795 to 1805, takes its impulse from Jauss's "Literary History as Challenge," but as will become apparent, my approach is more positivistic than Jauss's own practical criticism has been thus far.

THE GOTHIC READER

Let us turn to some results of a base-line study I have made of the reception of the Gothic novel in the decades bracketing the turn of the nineteenth century. The hypothesis that I am investigating, and which seems tentatively warranted by the data I have collected, is that the Gothic novel sits astride a major shift in the response of readers to literature, a shift (in Jauss's terms) from *catharsis* to *aisthesis*, or in basic English, a shift from reading for information, and for the sake of entry into a verisimilar world otherwise inaccessible to the reader, toward reading as an escape from the world one inhabits into an inward locus of fantasy.

My research thus validates Q. D. Leavis's ideological argument, in *Fiction and the Reading Public*, that the reader of fiction has changed in character and motivation since the days of Fielding and Richardson — with the result that much of the modern public is baffled by Woolf and Joyce.[7] Leavis assigns various dates to this shift between 1770, with Charles Jenner's *The Placid Man*, and 1845, with the novels of Bulwer-Lytton, because for her own political point, the exact date does not matter. I would date the significant shift in response within these parameters, close to the turn of the nineteenth century. For my purposes, Leavis's categories of reader-response are too narrowly judgmental and too simplistic. Her distinction is merely between active and passive reading — with the former evaluated as good and the latter as bad; Leavis does not discriminate between one mode of activity or receptivity and another. From Jauss's point of view, however, *aisthesis* is as valid a mode of aesthetic experience as any other. In his framework, the active modes of reading demanded by *Tom Jones* and *Ulysses* or *Mrs. Dalloway* are not identical (as in Leavis's scheme) but different. Joyce and Woolf demand the reader's engagement in helping to *create* their narratives (Jauss's *poiesis*), whereas the engagement of the implied reader of Fielding has a very different *cathartic* function.

Despite these cavils, Leavis is surely correct that something important happened to the British reading public. What happened could be exemplified in the contrast between the reviews of Ann Radcliffe's *Mysteries of Udolpho* by the anonymous critic for the *Monthly Review* for 1794 and by Thomas Noon Talfourd in the *New Monthly Review* for 1820. In the former, Radcliffe is praised for her "correctness of sentiment and elegance of style," for her "admirable ingenuity of contrivance to awaken [the reader's] curiosity, and to bind him in the chains of suspense;" and for "a vigour of conception and a delicacy of feeling which are capable of producing the strongest sympathetic emotions, whether of pity or of terror."[8] These very same criteria of excellence are applied to *Udolpho* by the *Analytical Review* and *British Critic*, which praised the novel, as well as by the *Critical Review*, where the young Samuel Taylor Coleridge attacked it for *hyper*-ingenuity of contrivance.[9]

Contrast Talfourd: "When we read [Mrs. Radcliffe's romances], the world seems shut out, and we breathe only in an enchanted region where . . . the sad voices of the past echo through deep vaults and lonely galleries."[10] With Talfourd stands William Hazlitt, who in 1818 stated that Radcliffe "makes her readers twice children, and from the dim and shadowy veil which she draws over the objects of her fancy, forces us to believe all that is strange and next to impossible. . . . All the fascination that links the world of passion to the world unknown is hers, and she plays with it at her pleasure; she has all the poetry of romance, all that is obscure, visionary and objectless in the imagination."[11] It is not just the style of writing that is different here: the reviewers of 1794 are standing outside and evaluating a pretty fiction, while the later Talfourd and Hazlitt have entered inwardly into an imagined world.[12]

Their implicit notion that the object of literary art might be to move the reader to a state of ecstatic transport had been announced considerably earlier than *Udolpho*, when the Gothic vogue was just getting under way. In "On the Pleasure Derived from Objects of Terror" (1773), Anna Laetitia Aiken (later known as Mrs. Barbauld) explains thus the effect of the tale of horror: "A strange and unexpected event awakens the mind, and keeps it on the stretch; and where the agency of invisible beings is introduced . . . our imagination, darting forth, explores with rapture the new world which is laid open to its view, and rejoices in the expansion of its powers. Passion and fancy, cooperating, elevate the soul to its highest pitch; and the pain of terror is lost in amazement."[13] Years later Mrs.

Barbauld makes such claims, in favor of reading for the sake of escape and imaginative play, not merely for the Gothic but for novels in general: "The humble novel is always ready to enliven the gloom of solitude, . . . to take man from himself (at many seasons the worst company he can be in) and, while the moving picture of life passes before him, to make him forget the subject of his own complaints. It is pleasant to the mind to sport in the boundless regions of possibility; to find relief from the sameness of everyday occurrences by expatiating amidst brighter skies and fairer fields; to exhibit love that is always happy, valour that is always successful; to feed the appetite for wonder by a quick succession of marvellous events. . . ."[14]

This sense of the Gothic as demanding an inward projection, as carrying the reader toward states of transport and escape, appears not only in writers who favor and relish the state but in those who do not.[15] A close examination of the periodical literature in the latter decades of the eighteenth century, supplemented by the sources collected in John Tinnan Taylor's *Early Opposition to the English Novel*,[16] has led me to the conclusion that, where decriers of fiction had tended to suggest, in the 1760s and 1770s, that indiscriminate reading was likely to erode the moral principles, especially those of women, by providing poor examples of conduct, in the period after 1795 the anti-fiction pamphleteer was more likely to attack reading as something whose pernicious tendency acted by sapping strength of mind, wasting precious time, and calling the female reader into a world whose attractions would lead her to neglect the duties and pleasures of mere sublunary existence.

This change must be seen as a tendency rather than a revolution: nothing abruptly occurred in 1795. We can find moralists like John Bennett warning in 1789 that a passion for literature "is dangerous to a woman. It . . . inspires such a romantic turn of mind, as is utterly inconsistent with the solid duties and proprieties of life." Nor was this change permanent. In a generation or two, the pendulum was to swing back, for as Robert Colby has shown, the hostile reaction of the clergy to the sensation novels of the 1860s was a matter of their supposedly unwholesome influence on conduct rather than for sponsoring an evasion of the quotidian world in favor of an imaginary one.[17]

But it is clearly at the height of the Gothic vogue that "castle-building," the use of literature as material for fantasy, becomes the moralist's chief complaint. For example, one "Arietta," a self-styled "castle-builder," writes in to *Literary Leisure* to confess that she was in her youth "a great reader . . . so, what between studying Novels and inventing Moral tales for Magazines, my head was stored with marvellous adventures and hair-breadth 'scapes, such as I trusted to become the heroine of myself when time should have matured the grains still folded up in the bud of youth." Now having wasted that youth, she finds herself "at forty-seven, filling presently the same situation in the same family."[18] T. H., in *Lady's Monthly Museum*, writes about her daughter that she "reads nothing in the world but novels. I am afraid she will read herself into a consumption. . . . These time-killing companions monopolize every hour that is not devoted to dress or sleep. . . . I am afraid," she concludes, "that the girl will never get a husband," and she hopes the editor will suggest the name of a man willing to wed a beautiful and well-off young lady with the defect of an addiction to fiction.[19] On a more hysterical note, the *Sylph* for 6 October 1795, claims to have "actually seen mothers, in miserable garrets, *crying for the imaginary distress of an heroine*, while their children were *crying for bread*."[20] And one "Rimelli," writing on "Novels and Romances" for the *Monthly Mirror*, insists that "Romances . . . serve only to estrange the minds of youth (specially of females) from their own affairs and transmit them to those of which they read: so that, while totally absorbed with lamenting and condoling with the melancholy situation of . . . a Matilda . . . they neglect both their own interests and the several duties which they owe to parent, friend or brother. . . ."[21]

These are typical complaints from the last five years of the eighteenth century. Before the advent of the Gothic novel, in the 1760s and 1770s, the chief complaint of anti-novel preaching concerns fiction that, it was feared, would excite the amorous propensities of the young or provide them with poor examples of moral conduct—in short, the verdict of Johnson's *Rambler* 4.[22] Such moral objections do not entirely die out at the heyday of the Gothic: indeed the moralists were out in force at the appearance of *The Monk*.[23] But we begin to hear with increasing frequency a new cause of disapproval—distrust of the power of fiction to seduce the reader into an inward world. Around the turn of the nineteenth century this issue begins statistically to supersede those raised by Johnson.

The notion of such seduction by fiction appears, naturally enough, in the fiction of the period as well. The most famous fictional victim of the Gothic novel is Catherine Morland, the heroine of Jane Austen's *Northanger Abbey* (written in some form by 1803, though revised much later and not published until 1817, after Austen's death). It is Catherine who, after reading *The Mysteries of Udolpho*, mistakes a laundry list for a fragmentary manuscript, and takes General Tilney for an uxoricide, when he is in fact only the average snobbish and mercenary man of the world.

But Catherine is only one of a multitude of such victims of romance, whose pedigree goes back earlier in the eighteenth century to Charlotte Lennox's Arabella in *The Female Quixote* (1752) and Richard Brinsley

Sheridan's Lydia Languish in *The Rivals* (1775). Among the less well known is Sophia Beauclerc, of Mary Charlton's novel *Rosella, or Modern Occurrences*, published in 1799 by the same Minerva Press which furnished such Sophias and Catherines with their favorite reading. Sophia "could think and dream only on wild rocks and mountains, tremendous precipices, fringing woods, gushing cataracts, romantic cottages placed on acclivities and declivities, lovely Jacquelinas, Clarentinas, Rosinas, Emmelinas, and more humble Joannas, Susannas, Cicelies and Annas who inhabited them . . ., gazing at the pale moon which never fails to dart its silver beams through their humble casements with such uncommon brilliancy as to allow them to chuse by its pale light a favored poet from their libraries. . . ." After yielding to this elaborate fantasy — and the sentence I have been quoting in fact goes on for several pages — Sophia drags herself and her unacknowledged daughter off on a jaunt through Scotland and Wales "to explore the realms of romance." There in the boondocks, they are constantly making mistakes of the sort with which we are familiar, of losing touch with reality because their inner light sees only Gothic romance.[24]

Yet another example, probably read by Jane Austen, since she may be echoing the book at the beginning of *Northanger Abbey*, is *The Heroine, or the Adventures of Cherubina*, by Eaton Stannard Barrett (1813). Here Cherry Wilkinson, unhappily "doomed" as she says "to endure the security of a home, and the dullness of an unimpeached reputation,"[25] rechristens herself Cherubina de Willoughby and elopes to London in quest of the misfortunes and adventures that are the inevitable lot of the heroines of the romances to which she is addicted. Fortunately for this particular female Quixote, a young man who happens to be her father's choice for her husband is willing to play Sancho Panza and he eventually manages to shock her back into sanity again.

These fictions — to which we could also add Mary Brunton's *Self-Controul* (Edinburgh: 1811) — are obviously exaggerated portraits, but equally obviously they have to be based upon something real or the satire could not have been so common or current. One reason why, around the turn of the nineteenth century, the Female Quixote reappears frequently as a reader of the Gothic novel has to do with the feelings demanded of readers by the Gothic itself. I would claim the implied reader of the Gothic novel is a somewhat different being than the implied reader of Fielding and Smollett. The Gothic demands for its full effects — effects not only of terror but of sublimity — a less skeptical or self-contained mind-set and a more empathetic attitude than does comic realism.

These demands are implicit in the structure of suspense in Gothic novels. The implied reader of *The Mysteries of Udolpho*, for example, is expected to retain strong suspense about the secret concealed by the celebrated Black Veil, despite the fact that Emily, after her initial swoon, is not actively threatened by it. The implied reader of *The Monk* is expected to develop strong tension over the fate of Raymond at the hands of the Bleeding Nun — despite the fact that Raymond is himself narrating the story of the Nun and the Wandering Jew and has therefore lived to tell the tale. These anomalous structures of suspense presume an identification between the reader and the focal character that goes well beyond what serious narratives earlier in the century demanded. In a novel like *Tom Jones*, suspense is aroused only by episodes that directly touch the plot's central instabilities, while digressions off the main narrative line are structured not as suspense stories but as semi-independent apologues.

The reader's empathic stance is also implicit in the verbal texture and point of view typical of the Gothic novel. Coral Ann Howells has finely analyzed a passage from volume III, chapter vi of *Udolpho*, showing how the objective narrator, technically always present, disappears from view, so that the reader is forced to accept the ultimately vacuous imaginings and tergiversations of Emily at face value. And even Radcliffe's style contributes to the effect: "While the passage is cast in the form of reasoned argument, with one sentence depending on and balancing the other, it has really only the *appearance* of judiciousness; what we have in effect is the dramatisation of a process very close to obsession, going round and round the same point and finding no escape or release from the central anxiety" (Howells, pp. 54–55).

To be sure, one could claim that an empathic mind-set tightly focused upon the heroine's obsessions was nothing new. Something of the kind had been demanded of readers since midcentury, by Richardson's *Clarissa* and by some of the novels of the sentimental school, which were in some sense emotional sources of the Gothic. And yet if differences in quantity eventually make for differences in quality, if you would expect there to be a difference between the effects of *occasionally* watching a soap opera on television and watching soaps as a steady diet, then perhaps the Gothic novel had such an effect on a major segment of the British reading public.[26] That the addiction existed seems clear, not only from cautionary letters to women's magazines, but from documents like receipts from circulating libraries, which show one celebrated bluestocking going through fifty-five volumes of romance in the space of a month.[27]

The shifts in reading patterns I have marked here have been noted by other scholars, but they have not always been interpreted in the same way. In his immensely learned volume *The English Novel in the Magazines*, Robert D. Mayo concludes that "the criticism of prose fiction in the miscellanies . . . appears to be based not on compromise, but on contradiction. Motivated by an obvious desire to please the greatest number of potential readers, editors, directly or by implication, embraced all opinions on the English novel without worrying too much about consistency. The new fiction . . . was a serious threat to an ordered society . . .; it was also a delightful and profitable companion in idle hours, a useful guide to the social virtues, and part of the necessary equipment of every person of parts."[28] Mayo has closely observed the chaos and contradiction of opinions, but he seems to feel that the chaos is without any more significance than the editors' understandable desire to pander to their readership.

I think, to the contrary, that the split in the readership of magazines indicates something very significant, a shift in motives and in response. The grinding of moral and aesthetic gears that Mayo views as a meaningless noise signals to me — as gear-grinding sometimes does — the uncomfortable transition between two stable states. We can explain Mayo's contradictions by positing that in the 1790s there were two very different readers for whom writers wrote: one, whom clergymen and journalists of the age personified as older and male, who read primarily for factual information, for the reinforcement of ethical values, and for the pleasure of recognizing the persons and things of his world; a second, personified as younger and female, receptive rather than critical, and eager to indulge in what Akenside had lauded as "The Pleasures of the Imagination."

What I am suggesting is that the Gothic novel came in simultaneously with a new wave in reader response. In answer to the inevitable question — what caused what? — I would reply that the vogue of the Gothic probably functioned as both cause and effect. That is, the Gothic was able to develop as a genre owing to the ready-made presence of an audience segment already partially prepared, by Richardson, Prévost and the sentimental novelists, to read for imaginative play and escape. But the demands of the Gothic text upon the reader, not merely for suspension of disbelief but for an empathic participation in the perils and plight of the protagonists, reinforced the already growing shift in response. Furthermore, the Gothic vogue was partly self-generating, in that its popularity began to draw in new classes of reader which had not formerly been a significant part of the market for literature.

One major result was to pave the way for the reception of romanticism in poetry as well as fiction, with the result that English bards — Wordsworth, Byron, and Scott, at least — despite a bit of rough handling from Scotch reviewers, were able to stir without conspicuous resistance a public which already looked to literature for the play of fantasy, dream and desire. The second result was in the Gothic itself, which after 1810 tended to abandon the historical themes of Radcliffe and the German Schauerromantik in favor of the more explicitly fantastic imaginative worlds of Mary Shelley and Charles Robert Maturin. By then, the Gothic wave itself had already begun to recede, leaving in its ebb two masterpieces, *Frankenstein* (1818) and *Melmoth the Wanderer* (1820). By 1830 the genre had been temporarily exhausted from oversupply by professionals and amateurs alike. But the sensibility that it had created would carry over into the new historical romances of Scott and Bulwer-Lytton, Ainsworth and Reynolds, as well as the more contemporary romantic novels of Dickens and the Brontës. When the Gothic resurfaced once more in late Victorian times it would be against a very different literary and social backdrop.

METHODOLOGICAL ISSUES

At this point a number of questions arise about both the facts I have been using and the theoretical superstructure that would turn those facts into data. Some of these questions have satisfactory answers, but others unfortunately do not.

At the lowest level of theoretical interest are questions about the facts: what they mean and whether they mean anything. We need to ask how many facts it takes to make a proof, whether we should allow ourselves to be convinced by circumstantial evidence about how people read two hundred years ago, and how we can make a couple of trends add up to a cause-and-effect relationship.

The first issue turns on what the social scientists would call statistical significance. I have presented what amounts to a series of impressions suggesting a shift in the motives for reading in the late eighteenth century. But how does one measure such a trend? How much data is enough? I have here presented quotations and citations from dozens of eighteenth-century sources; I have examined in New York and London perhaps a few hundred more. This is a fair sample size, but I would have no idea when these impressions would acquire statistical significance. The sampling of sources I have located may also have been subtly skewed in ways I cannot allow for. The reader responses I have cited are certainly unusual in at least one respect: all of them managed to find their way into print, as most receptions surely do not.

A second issue, or set of issues, turns on what counts as a source. The Murphy's Law of reception-theory is that the most naive readers are the least likely to leave evidence of their response to texts. In six weeks at the British Museum I was able to turn up only a handful of diaries and letters in which the real-life counterparts of Catherine Morland gave some sense of the motivation and experiential value of their readings. Most diarists and correspondents never mentioned their reading; a few listed it; even fewer expressed the feelings that their reading inspired in them or the desires that inspired them to pick up a volume in the first place. But circumstantial evidence is still acceptable even in a court of law, and I feel reasonably confident that, when we find a trend among moralists to attack novel-reading as an activity that unfits young ladies and gentlemen for real life, rather than as a mirror of depraved manners, it suggests a real change in the way real people read novels. But one has to be cautious about drawing conclusions, for we could account for this trend in a number of other plausible ways—such as an upward valuation of sloth relative to lust as a deadly sin.

If we would prefer to look for a direct expression of response to fiction, the most obvious source would be the book reviews, especially the *Analytical*, *Critical*, and *European Reviews*, as well as the *British Critic* and the *Anti-Jacobin*. All these publications reviewed Gothic fiction at least from time to time, and I have read and collected most of these notices. As it happens, the sensibility that I hypothesize grew in the 1790s finds virtually no expression in these publications. The reviewers differ considerably in their taste and tolerance for Gothic fiction, but all of them tend to discuss the novel in neoclassical or Johnsonian terms, with an emphasis on the probability, generality and ethical probity of the narrative.[29] This is a blow to my hypothesis, and it may be that the trend toward *aisthesis* that I have discussed was a wholly factitious artifact of my data-collecting methods. But there are two alternative explanations.

One is that the trend toward *aisthesis* was unevenly spread among Jauss's levels of the audience—that it was visible on the top level of authors and the bottom level of common readers but not on the intermediate level of reviewers. It may sound implausible that such a revolution should have bypassed this quasi-elite group of *Kulturträger*, but there are two good reasons why it might *appear* that way. One has to do generally with the stance of the reviewer from that time to this: briefly, the requirement that one evaluate for a mass publication with rapid-fire deadlines a heavy pile of fiction is not likely to encourage a stance of revery and escape. The reviewer is not escaping the workaday world in reading: reading *is* the reviewer's workaday world. The second reason has to do very specifically with the structure and function of book reviews in magazines in the late eighteenth century. Anyone who peruses these reviews will be struck by how much space is devoted to lengthy summaries of the plot and even lengthier quotations from the books in question and how little to serious analysis of the works' attractions and deficiencies. The cause is spelled out by Robert Mayo: owing to a peculiarity of the copyright law of 1710, magazines "claimed, and were more or less accorded, the right to abridge, or print extracts from, any literary work irrespective of copyright. For more than a hundred years, consequently, British miscellanies enjoyed a kind of legalized piracy."[30] The implication of this is that reviewers of Gothic fiction understood their critiques as valuable less in themselves than as they constituted a licence for the lengthy semipiratical extract which took up most of the article. Such reviewers would be more likely to do the fast-and-dirty-hack job that their editors would be satisfied with, evaluating the novel in terms of traditional but irrelevant issues like probability (even the historical and topographical accuracy of the novels), rather than exploring with difficulty, and without much prior basis in critical theory, any shifts that may have occurred in their own sensibilities.

An alternative explanation, and the one I lean toward, is that the trend may have been limited, in the 1790s, to the middle-class women who made up much of the market for the Gothic novel, though it later spread across the gender gap to men, as my examples from Talfourd and Hazlitt suggest. Ina Ferris has given good reason to believe that one primary agent of the contagion — though not the only one — was the publication of Scott's *Waverley* in 1814. In a study of the reception of *Waverley*, Ferris has shown that the novel's masculine virtues (like historical factuality) not only pleased the male reviewers, but also seem to have licensed them to take pleasure in that novel's romantic qualities — romantic qualities that they might have been reluctant to praise, since they were otherwise felt to be characteristic of women's reading.[31] A male prejudice against what were perceived as female modes of reading might also account for the reviewers' inability to respond to the Gothic with a sensibility appropriate to romantic fiction. We cannot be sure why women should have been especially sensitive to this mode of aesthetic experience, though we might guess that increased leisure time without opportunities for useful work might conduce toward ennui, lassitude and desires for escape.[32]

In addition to the quantity and quality of the evidence, there is a question about which way the causal arrow points, if it points at all. To me it seemed reasonable to suppose that it pointed both ways, that the eighteenth-century reading public had been to an extent prepared for Radcliffe by Richardson, but that the Gothic novel itself had largely induced the trend toward *aisthesis* that we find everywhere by 1815. It might be argued — though with difficulty — that the emphasis should be reversed: that the Gothic was more the effect of a change in sensibility than its cause. But a skeptic might claim that no causal relation has been demonstrated at all, that I have merely made a *post hoc* argument about two trends, neither of which can even be placed in time with precision.[33]

The way is surely left open for orthodox Marxists to claim, for example, that both the Gothic novel as a form and the shift in the sensibility of its readership are connected only as the common result of changes in modes of economic production—such as the Industrial Revolution. David Punter has in fact argued this line, but it is the least convincing aspect of his otherwise excellent survey, *The Literature of Terror*. Still, Punter's failure would certainly not preclude greater success for a more subtle Marxist approach.[34]

Nevertheless, it must be understood that there are limits to the power of that approach. The customary advantage claimed by Marxist criticism over its rivals is that it appeals for its explanations to social and economic factors that are clearly broader than and prior to the texts under scrutiny. The corresponding disadvantage—which is seldom perceived and faced by its practitioners—is that the connections between economic cause and artistic effect that Marxists perceive are generally so tenuous that they need to be taken with a strong dose of faith. Marxist critics, despite a theoretical commitment to materialism, also tend to evade positivistic questions about the working of the literary marketplace, and instead refer questions about the causal relations of economic and artistic phenomena to the mystical mediation of "ideology." But in the long run, there need be no ultimate conflict between reception theory and Marxist criticism. The theories differ primarily in "focal length": reception theory stays closer to the text itself than Marxism but is narrower in its scope, while Marxism is broader but more distant. These theories are alike, however, in that they both seek to explain predisposing causes, causes that were necessary but not sufficient, that aided in the creation of literary texts.

CONCLUSION

After my theses about the reception of the Gothic in the 1790s—and its impact on the course of the Gothic novel and on Romanticism in general—have been qualified by the methodological questions I have just raised, the results may seem disappointingly tentative. One of the obvious difficulties about this method of establishing historical relationships is that, like most other sorts of historical research, it leads rather to a reassessment of probabilities and connections than to absolute certainties. That is because reception theory is not based upon an a priori theory, an ideology which is guaranteed to reconstitute the facts of the world according to its dictates. It is instead a positivistic method attempting to relate circumstances and actualities within the world — the world which consists of "everything that is the case:" What is the case is never a matter of mere logic.

Nevertheless, the suggestive probabilities that reception theory can provide are weakened somewhat by the fact that it is an art just past its infancy rather than one fully developed. It is true that the theorists have had their say over the last twenty years, as Jauss's theory has been attacked by Marxists and Formalists, and it has emerged refined and tempered from the fire of philosophical analysis. After twenty years, in fact, *Literary History as Challenge* no longer seems a revolutionary document; it has become a paradigm of the humanities. But it is just beginning to generate research analogous to what Thomas Kuhn called "normal science."[35]

But since this is just beginning, each individual researcher, working through piles of printed and manuscript evidence of literary reception, is forced to grope in the dark, to invent his methodology anew. Only as more studies of reception reach the stage of publication will the fragments begin to connect with one another and to build up a coherent diachronic portrait of the reading public. At times (as with Q. D. Leavis's study and my own), we should expect scholars to disagree on principles of explanation, which will need to be debated and clarified before a consensus will emerge. At other times — as with my work and that of Ina Ferris cited above — two researchers will find material that is complementary, where each holds part of the key to the other's problem.

Given the wide range of obscure sources that need to be consulted, it is unlikely that it will ever be possible to make a broad and general study of reception. Each researcher will be able to comprehend only a carefully delimited area of audience response. Thus, in the long run, the most difficult problem that we shall face is how to synthesize these fragmentary studies of reception into a picture large enough to be informative on a scale that we would call literary history — that is, not just a history of the Gothic novel but a history of the literature of a single nation — or, better still, of a continent of nations that have mutually influenced one another. But though a familiarity with literary theory will be required for such a task, this is work, not for professional theorists as such, but for practical critics who will solve these massive problems in the course of trying to say something true about the imaginative life of the past.

Notes

1 I am summarizing Hans Robert Jauss, "Literary History as a Challenge to Literary Theory," in *Toward an Aesthetics of Reception*, translated by Timothy Bahti (Minneapolis: University of Minnesota Press, 1982), pp. 3–46. I also wish to acknowledge that my essay was written with the generous support of the National Endowment for the Humanities.

2 For example, by René Wellek in "Zur methodischen Aporie einen Rezeptionsgeschichte," in *Geschichte: Ereignis und Erzählung*, eds. Reinhart Koselleck and Wolf-Dieter Stempel (München: Wilhelm Fink Verlag, 1973), p. 515.

3 Hans Robert Jauss, "Sketch of a Theory and History of Aesthetic Experience," in *Aesthetic Experience and Literary Hermeneutics* (Minneapolis: University of Minnesota Press, 1982), p. 10.

4 Hans Robert Jauss, "Theses on the Transition from the Aesthetics of Literary Works to a Theory of Aesthetic Experience," in *Interpretation of Narrative*, Mario J. Valdès and Owen Miller, eds. (Toronto: University of Toronto Press, 1978), pp. 138–46.

5 Hans Robert Jauss, "Theses on the Transition," p. 142–43. Jauss had suggested earlier (with vacuously circular logic) that the explicit reader might be inferred from the implied reader within the text: "There is also the possibility of objectifying the horizon of expectations in works that are historically less sharply delineated. For the specific disposition toward a particular work that the author anticipates from the audience can also be arrived at, even if explicit signals are lacking, through . . . familiar norms; through . . . the implicit relationships to familiar works of the literary-historical surroundings; and . . . through the reflective function of language." "Literary History as Challenge to Literary Theory," in *Toward an Aesthetic of Reception*, p. 24.

6 For example, how Valéry read Goethe's *Faust* or how Gautier, Huysmans, Valéry and Walter Benjamin read Baudelaire's "Spleen." See "Goethe's and Valéry's *Faust*: On the Hermeneutics of Question and Answer" and "The Poetic Text within the Change of Horizons of Reading: the Example of Baudelaire's 'Spleen II,' " in *Toward an Aesthetic of Reception*, pp. 110–185.

7 Q. D. Leavis, *Fiction and the Reading Public* (London: Chatto and Windus, 1932), pp. 135–150.

8 Review of *The Mysteries of Udolpho*, *Monthly Review*, n.s., 15 (November 1794): 278–83.

9 See "A. Y." in the *Analytical Review* 19 (June 1794): 140–45; *British Critic* 4 (August 1794): 110–121; *Critical Review* 11 (August 1794): 361–70.

10 T. Noon Talfourd, *Critical and Miscellaneous Writings* (London: T. Bell, 1852). Originally published in the *New Monthly Magazine* 14 (June 1820).

11 William Hazlitt. *Lectures on the English Comic Writers* (1818; London: J. M. Dent, 1890), p. 195.

12 The response to fiction that we see in Talfourd and Hazlitt was nevertheless

available to readers in the mid-eighteenth century. A glance at Henry Fielding's letter to Richardson after completing the first two parts of *Clarissa*
demonstrates that the author of *Tom Jones* was capable of projecting himself
psychically into Richardson's fiction with an intensity unrivalled by the
Gothic-besotted heroine of *Northanger Abbey* [for the letter, cf. F. Homes
Dudden, *Henry Fielding: His Life, Works, and Times* (Hampden, CT: Archon
Books, 1966) II: 719-20]. But it is interesting that the novel that calls up
that heated response in Fielding is the very one from which the Gothic novel
derived much of its emotional tone. See Coral Ann Howells, *Love, Misery
and Mystery* (London: Athlone, 1978), pp. 8, 26.

13 Anna Laetitia Barbauld, "On the Pleasure Derived from Objects of Terror,"
in J. and A. L. Aikin, *Miscellaneous Pieces in Prose* (3rd edn: London: 1792).

14 Anna Laetitia Barbauld, "On the Origin and Progress of Novel-Writing"
prefaced to *The British Novelists*, 50 vols. (London: F. C. and J. Rivington, et
al., 1810), p. 58.

15 For example, Coleridge in *Biographia Literaria* says of the devotees of the
Gothic novel: "I dare not compliment their *passtime*, or rather *kill-time* with
the name of reading. Call it rather a sort of beggarly daydreaming, during
which the mind of the dreamer furnishes for itself nothing but laziness and a
little mawkish sensibility; while the whole *materiel* and imagery of the doze is
supplied *ab extra* by a sort of mental *camera obscura* furnished in the printing
office, which *pro tempore* fixes, reflects and transmits the moving phantasms
of one man's delirium so as to people the barrenness of an hundred other
brains afflicted with the same trance or suspension of all common sense and
all definite purpose." S. T. Coleridge, *Collected Works*, ed. James Engell and
W. Jackson Bate, 16 vols. (Princeton: Princeton University Press, 1983), 7:
i: 48.

16 John Tinnan Taylor. *Early Opposition to the English Novel: The Popular Reaction
from 1760 to 1830* (New York: King's Crown Press, 1943).

17 The Rev. John Bennett, *Letters to a Young Lady* (1789; 7th American edition:
Philadelphia: Anthony Finley, 1818), p. 136. Robert A. Colby's work was
presented as an MLA talk on the Victorian Gothic ("Victorian Gothic: Echo
and Transformation") at the 1985 annual meeting. His evidence involves
works like the Rev. Francis Edward Paget's *Lucretia, or The Heroine of the
Nineteenth Century* (London: Joseph Masters, 1868), whose epilogue insists
that every decent person help "preserve the purity of the young by putting
them on their guard against the perusal of writings which sedulously pander
to the worst passions of our nature. . . ."

18 *Literary Leisure, or The Recreation of Solomon Saunter, Esq.*, 1, no. 42 (July 10,
1800): 129-40.

19 *Lady's Monthly Museum* 2 (1798): 218-20.

20 *Sylph*, no. 5 (October 6, 1795): 35-38.

21 *Monthly Mirror* 14 (August 1802): 81. For similar reports see the letter of
"Sylvester Hawthorne" in the Dublin *Flapper*, I, 44 (July 2, 1796): 173-75;
"On the Terrorist System of Novel-Writing" in *Monthly Magazine* 4 (August

1797): 102-4. On the other side, an article in the *Monthly Mirror* 4 (November 1797): 277-79, entitled "Novel-Reading a Cause of Female Depravity," takes the position that a woman whose mind is "enervated" by a course of novel-reading is likely not to be unfitted for life but to be seduced by any languourous young man. The immoral consequences of *weakness of mind* produced by reading is a favorite theme of the 1780s: we find it in Vicesimus Knox's 1784 *Essays: Moral and Literary* (2 vols; 2nd edn.; London: Edward and Charles Dilly, 1789), 2:189, where Sterne's sentimental imitators are blamed for lack of moral self-control among the young. Such a theme is not to be confused with the later attacks on castle-building.

22 See Hester Mulso Chapone, *Letters on the Improvement of the Mind* (1773; Boston: James B. Dow, 1834, p. 143), who insists great care be given in the selection for children's reading "of those *fictitious stories* that so enchant the mind, most of which tend to inflame the passions of youth." But Chapone also fears that the immoderate reader will become a female Quixote. See also Taylor, passim.

23 The moral reaction to *The Monk* was very intense. For a full survey of the contemporary attacks and defenses of Matthew G. Lewis and his novel, see André Parreaux, *The Publication of "The Monk": A Literary Event 1796-98* (Paris: Didier, 1960).

24 Mary Charlton, *Rosella, or Modern Occurrences: a Novel.* 4 vols. (London: Minerva Press, 1799), 1: 281-84.

25 Eaton Stannard Barrett, *The Heroine, or the Adventures of Cherubina* (3rd edition: 3 vols. London: Henry Colburn, 1815), 1: 14-15.

26 The reading public's access to the Gothic was enhanced around 1791 by the enterprising William Lane's innovation of *franchising* his Minerva Press circulating library to tradesmen seeking comparable profits in the provinces. See Dorothy Blakey, *The Minerva Press: 1790-1820* (London: The Bibliographical Society at the University Press, Oxford, 1939), p. 114.

27 See, for example, A. G. K. Lestrange, ed., *The Life of Mary Russell Mitford; Told by Herself in Letters to Her Friends* (2 vols. New York: Harper and Bros., 1870), 2: 34. Thomas Babington Macaulay also frequented regularly the Minerva Press's circulating library, and it is suggestive that (as a letter from his sister Hannah records) he read at least one romance closely enough to have kept a tally of how often the various characters fainted (which was pretty often). Cf. Amy Cruse, *The Englishman and His books in the Early Nineteenth Century* (London: George G. Harrap, 1930), p. 101-2.

28 Robert D. Mayo, *The English Novel in the Magazines: 1740-1815* (Evanston: Northwestern University Press, 1962), pp. 271-72.

29 Critiques of Gothic fiction based on factuality abound; see among dozens of possible examples: (1) Review of Mary Robinson, *Walsingham, or, the Pupil of Nature*, in *Anti-Jacobin Review* 1 (August 1798): 160-64; (2) *Isobel, or, the Orphan of Valdarno; a Florentine Romance, founded during the Civil Wars in Italy*, which is attacked for its improbability in *Annual Review and History of Literature* 1 (1002): 722-23 and praised for its fidelity to fact in *Flowers of Literature*

2 (1802): 452; (3) Review of *The Captive of Valence; or the Last Moments of Pius VI* in *Eclectic Review* 1 (June 1805): 424–25. Clearly some readers must have cared: Elizabeth Carter wrote in 1794 to Mrs. Montagu that she found Tschink's *Herman of Unna* "very dull, but it is interesting from giving what I suppose is a true account of that most horrid institution the Secret Tribunal" (Letter #283, *Letters from Mrs. Elizabeth Carter to Mrs. Montagu 1755–1800* [London: F. C. and J. Rivington, 1817], III: 341). And authors themselves sometimes felt it necessary to explain or justify their departures from fact; Francis Lathom's introduction to *The Unknown; or the Northern Gallery* distinguishes for the audience between the imagined and the real events that his romance mixes together. Cf. review in *The Cabinet* 3 (April 1808): 189–90.

30 Robert D. Mayo, "The Gothic Romance in the Magazines," *PMLA* 65 (January 1950): 766–67.

31 Ina Ferris, "The Reception of the Waverley Novels," unpublished paper read April 1986 at the Conference on Narrative Poetics, in Columbus, Ohio.

32 I have suggested that at least the *bourgeois* reader was affected, but controversy persists over how far down in the social scale the addiction to Gothic fiction went. Sources like James Lackington's memoirs suggest that the reading of fiction was nearly universal. On the other hand, the price of books or of subscriptions to the circulating libraries was very high (the annual guinea for the Minerva Library subscription would be a good fraction of a footman's wage). Still, Altick reminds us that "if we are to believe the constant burden of contemporary satire, domestic servants attended [circulating libraries] in great numbers on their own account, not merely to exchange books for their mistresses." Richard Altick, *The English Common Reader: A Social History of the Mass Reading Public 1800–1900* (Chicago: University of Chicago Press, 1957), p. 62.

33 My argument rests on the usual dating of the beginning of the vogue of the Gothic in the early 1790s, rather before the series of attacks on castle-builders and Quixotes begins in the late 1790s and 1800s. But not only is my dating of the trend toward *aisthesis* necessarily vague, so is any dating of the vogue of the Gothic. See Robert D. Mayo, "How Long Was Gothic Fiction in Vogue?" *MLN* 58 (January 1943): 58–64, for some of the problems in making such estimations. Mayo's conclusion that the Gothic novel was essentially passé by 1814 seems questionable in the light of Ann Tracy's *The Gothic Novel 1790–1830* (Lexington: University Press of Kentucky, 1981). If we date the 208 novels analyzed and summarized in Tracy's volume, we find there was a short hiatus during 1813–17, but that the trend picked up again in the period 1818–22 before declining once more toward 1830. Mayo picks up the hiatus, but since he ends his study in 1820 he misses the brief recrudescence of the Gothic a few years later. Cf. my "The Gothic Impulse," *Dickens Studies Annual* 11 (1983): 287.

34 David Punter, *The Literature of Terror: A History of Gothic Fictions from 1765 to the Present Day* (London: Longman, 1980). It can be a great temptation to

move directly from a social or economic phenomenon to the literary text which reflects it, rather than, as Jauss would suggest, mediating the change through the audience which responds both to social realities and to texts. Punter uses the direct, Lukácsian method. His final chapter, which attempts to draw together the fragmentary social comments presented during his history, tends to mumble a great deal, to present ideas as rhetorical questions rather than as statements accompanied by evidence, and to base his literary trends on factitious or misunderstood social phenomena. For example, the frequent issue of rape in Gothic fiction is seen as a reaction to "the Augustan denial of the passions," a state of affairs which would have surprised many passionate Augustans (p. 416). But the post-Althuserrian version of Marxist literary analysis, which, like Jauss's reception theory, takes literature as a "relatively autonomous" practice of ideology, seems a more promising methodology. For a discussion of the confluence between reception theory and post-Althusserian Marxism in recasting the history of the Gothic novel, see my essay "The Unguarded Prison" in *The Eighteenth Century: Theory and Interpretation*, forthcoming 1989.

35 Thomas Kuhn, *The Structure of Scientific Revolutions* (2nd edition; Chicago: University of Chicago Press, 1966).

CONTRIBUTORS

JERRY C. BEASLEY is Professor of English at the University of Delaware. He is the author of *Novels of the 1740s* (Georgia, 1982) and is General Editor of *The Works of Tobias Smollett* (Georgia, in progress). Presently he is writing a book on Smollett's novels and conducting research for a book on Women of Letters in Eighteenth-Century England.

JOHN DUSSINGER is Professor of English at the University of Illinois. He is the author of *The Discourse of the Mind in Eighteenth-Century Fiction* (Mouton, 1974) and of numerous articles and reviews. He has recently completed a book manuscript on Jane Austen.

MITZI MYERS teaches at the University of California (Los Angeles) and Scripps College. She has published numerous essays and reviews on eighteenth- and nineteenth-century women writers and has received several research awards. She is presently working on a study of Georgian women writers of children's and educational books.

JOHN RICHETTI is Leonard Sugarman Professor of English at the University of Pennsylvania. His most recent books are *Philosophical Writing: Locke, Berkeley, Hume* (Harvard, 1983) and *Daniel Defoe* (Twayne, 1987). He is currently at work on a history of the British eighteenth-century novel and a survey of nonfictional prose in the period.

DAVID RICHTER, Professor of English at Queens College, is the author of *Fable's End* (Chicago, 1975), *Forms of the Novella* (New York, 1981), and *The Critical Tradition* (Boston, 1988). With the assistance of a grant from the National Endowment for the Humanities, he is currently at work on a book-length study of the Gothic novel and reception-theory.

ROBERT W. UPHAUS, Professor of English at Michigan State University, is the author of *The Impossible Observer* (Kentucky, 1979), *Beyond Tragedy* (Kentucky, 1981), and *William Hazlitt* (G. K. Hall, 1985). He is presently writing a book-length study of the early reception of the eighteenth-century English novel.

JOEL WEINSHEIMER is Professor of English at the University of Minnesota. He is the author of *Imitation* (Routledge & Kegan Paul, 1984) and of *Gadamer's Hermeneutics* (Yale, 1985), as well as numerous articles on eighteenth-century literature and critical theory.

INDEX